pulpo
paris fashion shopping

Pulpo Guides

Pulpo Paris Fashion Shopping Guide

Published by Pulpo Guides, an imprint of Pulpo Publishing

Copyright © 2002 by Pulpo Publishing

First edition, October 2002

Editor: Nina Granberg-Melin

Cover design: Camilla Lundsten

Printed in Sweden by Mediaprint

ISBN: 91-970325-1-4

Find us at **www.pulpoguides.com**

To buy our books

Pulpo Guides are distributed to book shops all over the world. They are also available for purchase at www.pulpoguides.com. Bulk purchases (10+ copies) of Pulpo Guides are available to corporations, organisations and institutions at special discounts and can be customised to suit individual needs. For more information, please contact Pulpo Publishing.

Over the last couple of years Paris has once again become the world's fashion hot spot, with new influences and spirit added to an unparalleled tradition of fashion. As well as that, the city also offers great shopping convenience. Especially if you take the time to understand the geography and what each area has to offer.

That's the reason why you should use this guide. Pulpo Guides aims to create a better experience in travel, shopping and eating. We believe every hour counts on your holiday and that every euro spent should offer you best value possible. Therefore you really should do some reading before getting into the jungle.

Pulpo would like to send a special thanks to Alicia Drake, the author of "A shopper's guide to Paris fashion", who pioneered the writing of good guides to fashion shopping. Your book has contributed a lot to the shopping experiences of the Pulpo crew and been a source of inspiration for us.

October 2002,
The Pulpo Crew

Always, visit: www.pulpoguides.com

Contents

About this book

This guide is about fashion shopping in Paris. We want to bring you the very best of the city's fashion scene in every price range and every style. Whether you are a heavy fashion junkie knowing everything there is to know about trends and labels, or just someone who wants to dress appropriately - this book is for you.

Every shop has been investigated by our devoted and experienced research team. Only the best in each category makes it into the guide. And since all of the researchers are fashion shopaholics and Paris-lovers that means the demands that have been set are high.

The guide is based on geographical areas, since that's the way we shop: If, for example, you are in the 6th arrondissement, or plan to go there, you will most likely want to know what's round the corner or on the next street. Every shop, therefore, is marked out on a fresh map. But if you are looking for a specific shop or label you can easily find it in the alphabetical index.

Every label or designer is listed where its main store or one of its shops is located. A label's main entry always ends with a listing of its other branches. The branches are also listed in their respective area with a reference to the label's main entry if more information is needed.

Each chapter starts with a short overview of what the area has to offer shopping-wise. The focus is on women- and menswear including shoes and accessories. But there is also a good selection of children's clothes, second-hand or vintage clothes, beauty products, and designer sale-shops.

There are two parts to each shop entry. The first part contains all the hard facts, such as address, telephone number, opening hours and nearest Metro station. Letters indicate what type of garment the store mainly sells. **W** is for womenswear, **M** is for menswear. **C** is for children's clothes. **A** is for accessories, B is for beauty products. **L** is for Lingerie, and **O** is for other.

Each entry also has a price indication. Since what some regard as cheap, others don't, this is no exact science, rather an indication of what to expect. € is for budget fashion, the high-street chains are typically found in this category. €€ indicates mid-priced clothing, ranging from more expensive high-street fashion to more affordable designer labels such as Hugo Boss and Max-Mara. €€€ is for the top-end of the market, or what most of us refer to as "luxury labels".

The second part of each entry is supposed to give you an idea of the style of the shop and/or designer. The intention is that every reader should get something out of it – regardless of his or her background knowledge.

Since even the most devoted shopper can't survive on shopping alone, we have also included our favourite stylish hotels, bars, restaurants and cafés. They are also listed by geographical area.

Normally Paris guide books are using the 20 different "arrondissements" to structure the information. However, these mainly legislative areas don't always reflect the way we shop. Therefore this book is structured slightly differently. The first chapter – "St- Honoré" – covers the streets along the rue Saint Honoré from Palais Royale to rue St-Florent, all in the first arrondissement. The second chapter – "Étienne Marcel-Les Halles" – covers the eastern part of the first arrondissement and the southern parts of the second. In the third chapter the third and fourth arrondissements join forces under the label "Le Marais". The fourth chapter – "St-Germain" – includes the sixth and seventh arrondissements. "Montaigne-Fbg St Honoré", the fifth chapter, covers the eighth arrondissement while "Opéra" includes the southwest of the ninth arrondissement and the western parts of the second. Passy-Victor Hugo covers the two most important shopping areas in the 16th arrondissement. The last chapter, Other Destinations, includes smaller areas in the 10th, 11th, 12th, 17th, and the 18th.

Every effort has been made to ensure that the information in this book is as up-to-date as possible at the time of going to print. However, the fashion shopping scene is changing. Therefore, if you should find that a shop or another venue has gone out of business or is not as it should be, please drop an e-mail to the editor@pulpoguides.com to let us know – we would very much appreciate it. This kind of news, as well as information about new shops and other Paris essentials will be published on our website www.pulpoguides.com. Check it out for up-to-date information about the wonderful world of travel, fashion, food and lifestyle.

But now, get ready, charge up your credit card, put on your comfiest shoes and get going! Paris is there waiting for you, and this guide will help you find some of its treasure, we can assure you of that. Enjoy!

Practical information

Opening hours

In general the shops are open between 10.00-19.00 every day, except Sundays. Some open a little bit later, and some don't close until 20.00. Nowadays most shops are open on Mondays and at lunchtime, although a few small ventures still close. More usually, many small shops open later on Mondays, so be sure to check the guide when you are planning to do your shopping tour. Sunday shopping is difficult in Paris. Some larger outlets like Virgin Megastore are open, but the big department stores are not. The most interesting Sunday shopping alternative is the Marais where many shops are open in the afternoon. The same goes for night shopping, only a few rare shops like Sephora and Virgin Megastore on the avenue des Champs Elysées stay open until midnight.

Holidays

Don't plan a serious shopping tour in August. Many small boutiques and restaurants close for a couple of weeks or even the whole month. Shops are normally closed on bank holidays. Check in advance.

Sales/Best time to shop

There are laws regulating when the sales ("soldes" in French) can take place. The first Monday after Christmas and the last week in June are the normal starting points, but it varies year to year, so be sure to check in advance, the tourist offices should be able to tell you. Toward the end of the sales, which normally last six weeks, some stores will advertise "deuxième démarque" or "dernière démarque" indicating further markdowns in price. Otherwise the best time to shop in Paris is in March and October when the ready-to-wear shows are on. The new collections have just arrived, and the city is full of fashion pros.

Alterations

Normally this is part of the service when you are buying fashion in Paris. What does vary is wether or not you are charged. The more exclusive the boutique, the more likely it is that alterations are done for free. Often the shop can speed the process up, if you're only in town for a short time, but you won't get it done in one day.

Etiquette and service

The level of service is normally high in French fashion boutiques. So high, actually that for many foreigners it can feel a bit annoying when the sales-person is right behind you following your every move. Don't get upset however, she is just trying to do her job. In the big high-street shops and department stores, you won't find that a problem. When you enter a shop you will always be greeted with a polite "Bonjour Madame" or "Bonjour Monsieur" and you are expected to say the same in reply. This also goes for when you're leaving; the shop assistants say "Au-revoir", and you should do the same.

Prices

Today the French franc has given way to the euro, which makes shopping and price comparison between European countries so much easier. Your experience of the prices in general for fashion in France depend, of course, on the prices in you own country, but to compare the three most important European fashion cities: London is the most expensive, Paris is somewhere in the middle and Milan is the best pricewise.

Getting around

The best way to conquer Paris is by underground (mètro in French). It's fast, it's cheap and you can go almost everywhere in the central parts of the city. Buy a tourist ticket for one or three days and you can travel as much as you want. You can also buy a "Carnet de dix", ten coupons which give you ten trips with no time constraints. At night a taxi is the best bet, the underground closes around midnight.

Nobody does it better. Over the last five years Paris has undergone a remarkable transformation, with a new energy vitalizing every part of it.

Just walking the streets you notice the atmosphere is quite different today than it was in the mid 1990s. Funky bars, new trendy restaurants, and of course the flourishing fashion scene, the city is more bustling than ever, with a new groove in the air.

When it comes to fashion, Paris has a unique position today. Drawing from the city's highly esteemed couture traditions the fashion houses standards of craftsmanship and bon goût is unparalleled in the world. Add to that a new generation of designers that have a more relaxed approach to fashion, wanting it to be excitingly fun, but at the same time wearable. The designers of today are also so much more in tune with the times, taking inspirations from every aspect of cultural life and every corner of the world, epitomised by British designer John Galliano's "we-wear-the world" collections for Dior.

Dior is also a good example of how many of the venerable French fashion houses over the last couple of years have undergone a much-needed face-lift. The trend is to enlist a new talented designer to breathe new life into a stodgy label. Marc Jacobs at Louis Vuitton, Tom Ford at YSL, Olivier and Michele Chatenet at Leonard, and Nicholas Ghesquière at Balenciaga are some of the best examples.

At the same time young independent designers are also making their mark, bringing forward collections that in the best cases are avant-garde and forward looking, and at the same time commercial enough to please the customers.

In the lower price category, the range of high-street chains – both French and international – has expanded. Today the supply of nice-price takes on the seasonal key trends makes it easy to up-date your wardrobe without paying a fortune.

The shopping experience itself has also never been better. The concept-store trend that Colette kick-started in 1997, has given us convenient mini-department stores, with all the indispensable items needed for that cool magazine lifestyle, all displayed in creative new ways. The big designer labels are battling against each other to create the biggest and most plush flagship store. The traditional department stores are getting revamped with modern new interiors and well-edited label mixes. The little personal boutiques also keep up, with the highest standards of service, and cool interiors as Jaques Le Corre and Alain Tondowski show. Shops with an edgy clubby feeling add further to the atmosphere.

For Paris shoppers this exciting diversity can easily be explored. Almost every arrondissement is literally a city within the city, with its own character and features. Fancy a small-town feeling with original little shops – go to the Marais. In search for young talents and alternative funky fashion go to the 10th, 11th, 12th and 18th arrondissement. Want deluxe designer wear? Then super-elegant avenue Montaigne and it's 8th arrondissement surroundings won't let you down. To sum it up when talking Parisian fashion, there is something for everybody regardless of taste, time constraints or budget.

Add to all of this a timeless beauty and grandeur that few other cities possess and it's easy to see why Paris is more than ever the capital of fashion.

1

St Honoré

For that cool and trendy fashion shopping experience the 1st arrondissement is an absolute must.

With Colette, Maria Luisa, and Chanel as the fashion reference points, the area consisting of rue St-Honoré and rue Cambon is rightly called the golden fashion triangle. Today it's one of the hottest spots for big designer labels looking to open plush new flagship stores.

The 1st arrondisment is situated on the Rive Droite, the right bank of the river Seine. It's characterised by the world's largest art museum the Louvre and the Tuilleries gardens. In many ways the atmosphere is that of the official capital, with all its grandeur and imposing mansions. Every tourist that visits Paris probably ends up here sooner or later. Here you'll also find the beautiful Palais Royal, designed by Richelieu in the 17th century, a lesser-known gem, perfect for a moment of tranquility.

Strolling in the narrow rue St-Honoré and rue Cambon don't be surprised when almost every person you meet is dressed like they just stepped out of that glossy magazine of yours. You're now in one of the hippest shopping areas in Paris. Since 1997 when Colette, the reference spot for cool concept-stores opened up here, the area's level of fashion cred has risen considerably.

Chanel's flagship store, a Parisian fashion institution, is on rue Cambon. Here as well you have Maria Luisa's empire, with four boutiques selling cutting-edge designer labels; and since 2002 a fifth; a whole store dedicated to the famous shoebrand Manolo Blahnik. Also, Italian designer Ennio Capasa's Costume National has headed for rue Cambon, opening its first Parisian outlet during the autumn 2002. And only a stone's throw from here, in rue Montpensier, the Belgian avantgarde designer Martin Margiela has opened his third outlet after Brussels and Tokyo. If you take rue Castiglione you end up at the elegant Place Vendôme, where all the most prestigious jewellery houses like Cartier, Dior, Chaumet, and Bulgari are gathered.

In the 1st arrondissement you'll also find Les Halles, but as it's most convenient to include it in a shopping-tour of the second arrondissement, you'll find it together with the Étienne Marcel quarters in the next chapter.

Eating and drinking

Cabaret
2, place du Palais-Royal
01 58 62 56 25

This venue is part of the booth trend that at the moment dominates the Paris restobar scene, and it has quickly become a top place in town. The Costes-inspired food is well executed.

Willi's Wine Bar
13 rue des Pétits-Champs
01 42 61 05 09

A classic hang-out, a perfect place to stop before or after a meal. They also serve great food.

Café Marly
93 rue de Rivoli
01 49 26 06 60

One of Paris' most striking restaurant settings, facing the Louvre pyramid. Perfect for a drink, or meal whenever. Try their breakfast!

Macéo
15 rue des Pétits-Champs
01 42 97 53 85

Charming restaurant close to the Palais Royal with a mix of contemporary and classic French cooking with a touch of haute cuisine.

Le Fumoir
6 rue de l'Amiral-de-Coligny
01 42 92 00 24
www.lefumoir.com

A stylish crowd frequents the bar and the library is the perfect place for browsing the papers.

Staying

Hôtel Costes
239 rue St-Honoré
01 42 44 50 00
www.hotelcostes.com

After seven years Hôtel Costes still draws the jet-set. The super cool pool (Paris' best?) with music playing underwater is a must. Expect to pay around €600 for a double.

Hôtel Ritz
15, place Vendôme
01 43 16 30 30
www.ritz.com

The legendary Ritz has been the place to stay for celebs like Coco Chanel and Marcel Proust. Lady Di and Dodi had their last supper here. It has all the glitz a palace hotel is supposed to have. Doubles start at €680.

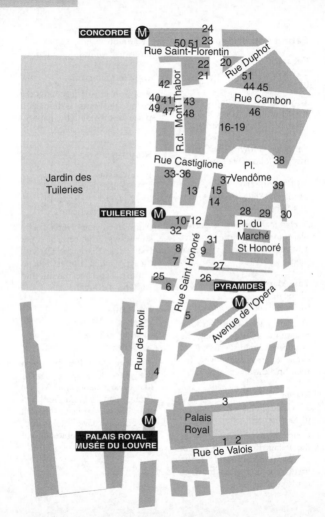

Gallerie de Valois
1. Les Salons du Palais -
   Royal Shiseido

Rue de Valois
2. Jerôme l'Huillier

Rue de Montpensier
3. Martin Margiela

Rue Saint Honoré
4. Hugo
5. Shiatzy Chen
6. Jacques Le Corre
7. Marcel Marongiu
8. Colette
9. Coccinelle
10. Céline et Jeanne
11. Stephane Marais
12. Mandarina Duck
13. Church's
14. Gucci
15. Boss Sport
16. Christian Lacroix
17. Ermenegildo Zegna
18. Hugo Boss
19. Valentino
20. BCBG
21. MaxMara
22. Ventilo
23. Georges Rech
24. Joseph

Rue St-Roch
25. Cabane de Zucca
26. Pallas

Rue de la Sourdière
27. Éric Bergère

Place de la Marché St Honoré
28. Espace Comme de Garçons
29. JC de Castelbajac
30. Philippe Model

Rue du Marché St-Honoré
31. Corinne Cobson

Rue du 29 Juillet
32. Zadig et Voltaire

Rue de Castiglione
33. Claude Litz
34. Annick Goutal
35. Rudolphe Menudier
36. Bleu Comme Bleu

Place Vendôme
37. Giorgio Armani
38. Emporio Armani
39. Charvet

Rue Cambon
40. Maria Luisa
41. Maria Luisa Accessories
42. Costume National
43. Tiki Tirawa
44. Apostrophe
45. Chanel
46. Fifi Chachnil

Rue Mont Thabor
47. Maria Luisa Homme
48. Maria Luisa Mixte

Rue Rivoli
49. D&G

Rue Saint-Florentin
50. Junko Shimada/Junk
51. Nina Gill

Rue Duphot
52. Victoire

1. Les Salons du Palais-Royal Shiseido – Scent

25, rue de Valois   M° Louvre-Rivoli
01 49 27 09 09   Mon-Sat 09.00-19.00
B   €€€

The luxurious setting of the Palais-Royal is perfect for Japanese Shiseido's perfume palace. Designer and perfumer, Serge Lutens, has dreamt-up this unique place that takes luxury in shop interiors to new levels. The most exquisite materials like marble and rosewood, the brilliant architecture with it's marble floors, and the staircase that unrolls in a curl of copper and bronze, blend together with the enchanting multi-note fragrances like Tuberose Criminelle and Bois de Violette. Each of them of course comes in the legendary bottles that can also be engraved upon request.

2. Jerôme L'Huillier - French Cocktail-Chic

27, rue de Valois   M° Palais-Royal M. d. Louvre
01 49 26 07 07   Mon-Sat 11.00-19.00
W   €€

Jerôme L'Huillier takes his inspiration from the movie-world, with a fashionable ultra-feminine cocktail-chic style. Brilliant colour combinations like plum, lilac and pink, or turquoise, khaki and camel are printed on silk, mesh and crepe. The look is easy-to-wear, safe fashion, as in his most famous items – the perfectly cut dresses.

2. Martin Margiela - Avantgarde Designer Wear

25 bis, rue Montpensier   M° Palais-Royal M. d. Louvre
01 40 15 07 55   Mon-Sat 11.00-19.00
A W M   €€€

When Martin Margiela opened this all-white store in 2002 he was the first member of the famous group of Antwerp designers to open a Parisian own-label-store. Margiela is very much of an avantgarde artist using deconstruction and recycling of vintage clothes or any material he will find suitable. Lately he has shown collections in bright colours in a rather playful mood.

4. Hugo - Hugo Boss Trendy Line

165, rue Saint Honoré
01 42 60 68 29
M W

M° Palais-Royal M. du Louvre
Mon-Sat 10.00-19.00
€€

Hugo is the youngest and trendiest of the Boss labels. For more details see Montaigne-Fbg St-Honoré.

5. Shiatzy Chen - Taiwanese Designer

262, rue Saint Honoré
01 40 15 95 98
W

M° Tuileries
Mon-Sat 10.00-19.00
€€

This minimalistic boutique, designed by architect Odile Becq is the first European one for Taiwanese Shiatzy Chen. The label, famous in designer Wang Chen's home country, is made up of beautiful East-meets-West clothes. A lustrous fusion of Chinese colours and prints with modern clean cuts.

6. Jacques Le Corre - Designer Accessories

193, rue Saint Honoré
01 42 96 97 40
A

M° Concorde
Mon-Sat 10.00-19.00
€€€

The milliner Jacques Le Corre has worked with all the major fashion houses such as Chloé, Jil Sander and Kenzo. Now, under his own label he also makes bags, shoes and boots in his personal elegant style. Exclusive materials, clean shapes and up-to-date colours make this a must for accessories-addicts in search of a change from all the big designer labels.

7. Marcel Marongiu - Hip Designer Wear

203, rue Saint Honoré
01 49 27 96 38
W

M° Tuileries
Mon-Sat 10.30-19.30
€€€

Franco-Swedish designer Marcel Marongiu's clothes are all about urban modernity with a sexy edge. He reinvents the classics, giving them a hip look whether it be a narrow suit, long skirt or slim trousers. Lycra is the key fabric and he mixes it with cotton, jersey, wool and silk, for a slim but comfortable silhouette. The palette is always sober and wearable with black, shades of brown and skin tones.

8. Colette - Fashion Concept Store

213, rue Saint Honoré   M° Tuileries
01 55 35 33 90   Mon-Sat 10.30-19.30
A B M W O   €€€

Colette, the mega-success of the late 1990s in fashion retailing, has set the standard for all the concept-stores that have followed. Nowadays, although not as ground-breaking anymore, the concept still draws the crowds with an ongoing quest for the new and hip; may it be clothes, home furnishings, shoes, magazines or accessories. The mix of hottest international designer labels and newcomers is a perfect mirror of the season's key trends. Everything is picked according to certain seasonal store themes and is displayed in a way that resembles a museum. Check out the beauty counter for Kiehl's and Nars. Downstairs the water bar, offering more than 30 different brands of bottled water, is the perfect lunch stop.

9. Coccinelle - Fashionable Accessories

326, rue Saint Honoré   M° Tuileries
01 44 55 32 11   Mon-Sat 10.00-19.00
A   €€

Italian accessories company Coccinelle successfully makes handbags and shoes that have the right dose of fashion to attract a wide range of women. Their collection of different shapes and styles nod at all major trends be it colourful flowers, sporty canvases or logoprints. Good value for money.

10. Cécile et Jeanne - Jewellery

215, rue Saint Honoré   M° Tuileries
01 42 61 68 68   Mon-Sat 11.00-20.00
A   €€

In a colourful baroque setting, Cécile and Jeanne display luxurious and unconventional accessories in exuberant forms inspired by modern art. The choice of materials reigns supreme with lapis-lazuli, pewter and brass mixing with crystal or bronze. *Also at: 12, rue des Francs Bourgeois (Le Mararis), 4, rue de Sèvres (St-Germain)*

11. Stephane Marais - Cosmetics

217, rue Saint Honoré   M° Palais-Royal M. du Louvre
01 42 61 73 22   Mon-Sat 10.30-19.30
B   €€

What first catches your eye when looking at celebrity make-up artist Stephane Marais brand new skincare and make-up range is the fresh take on the packaging. "It's the mascot of the collection" Marais states of the collages of graffiti art, city silhouettes, snapshots and weird statements that change every three months. Marais, formerly the head of Shiseido's Clé de Peau cosmetic line, has come up with over 100 products such as an astonishing new mascara pencil, and every few months new items will be released.

12. Mandarina Duck - Modern Luggage & Clothes

219, rue Saint Honoré   M° Tuileries
01 42 60 76 20   Mon-Sat 10.00-19.00
A M W   €€

This Italian label, best known for it's smart luggage, also does men and womenswear with a sporty travel-friendly urban look. The colours and fabrics are innovative, and so is the interior at the Droog-designed St Honoré concept-store where the clothes are lashed to the walls with baggage straps of different colours, for example. *Also at: 51, rue Bonaparte, (St-Germain), 7 boulevard de la Madeleine, (Opéra).*

13. Church's - Classic Men's Shoes

227, rue Saint Honoré   M° Tuileries
01 55 35 34 60   Mon-Sat 10.00-19.30
A M   €€€

Though it was taken over by the Prada group in 1999, Church's is still the quintessential English shoe shop. Made of the finest leather, with quality craftsmanship and the trademark Good Year-welded sole, the 130 year old British shoemaker is the choice for discerning men wanting good old-fashioned Oxford lace-ups or buckle shoes. With Prada in the boardroom, though, there have been some changes like the relaunch of the penny loafer – it was their second-best seller in the year 2001. *Also at: 4, rue Dragon (St-Germain).*

14. Gucci - Bags, Shoes and Accessories

350, rue Saint Honoré   M° Concorde
01 42 96 83 27   Mon-Sat 10.00-19.00
A   €€€

At this store you find accessories. For details see Montaigne - Fbg St-Honoré.

15. Boss Sport - Leisure Menswear

352, rue Saint Honoré   M° Concorde
01 42 60 57 93   Mon-Sat 10.00-19.30
M   €€

For details see Montaigne - Fbg St-Honoré.

16. Christian Lacroix - French Couturier

366, rue Saint Honoré   M° Madeleine
01 42 61 39 08   Mon-Sat 10.00-19.00
A M W   €€€

For details see Montaigne - Fbg St-Honoré.

17. Ermenegildo Zegna - Italian Tailoring

368, rue Saint Honoré   M° Concorde
01 42 60 95 86   Mon-Sat 10.00-19.00
M   €€€

For details see Montaigne - Fbg St-Honoré.

18. Hugo Boss - Modern Men and Womenswear

374, rue Saint Honoré M° Concorde
01 47 03 40 53 Mon-Sat 10.00-19.00
M W €€

For details see Montaigne - Fbg St-Honoré.

19. Valentino - Italian Couturier

376, rue Saint Honoré M° Concorde
01 42 60 40 26 Mon-Sat 10.00-19.00
M €€€

Here you'll find menswear. For details see Montaigne - Fbg St-Honoré.

20. BCBG - Trend Men and Womenswear

412-414, rue Saint Honoré M° Concorde
01 40 20 16 50 Mon-Sat 10.00-19.30
AWM €€

For details see Opéra.

21. MaxMara - Italian Elegant Womenswear

265, rue Saint Honoré M° Concorde
01 40 20 04 58 Mon-Sat 10.30-19.00
A W €€

For details see Montaigne - Fbg St-Honoré.

22. Ventilo - French Classic Womenswear

267, rue Saint Honoré M° Concorde
01 40 15 61 52 Mon-Sat 10.00-19.00
W €€

For details see Étienne Marcel - Les Halles.

23. Georges Rech - French Chic

273, rue Saint Honoré
01 42 61 41 14
W M

M° Concorde
Mon-Sat 10.00-19.00
€€€

This is certainly not for those seeking that big fashion statement. What Georges Rech can supply you with is high-quality classic clothes. The wide range of dresses, trousers and coats look good and fit perfectly. The men's suits are among the highlights; the look is well-dressed in a conservative way. Rather expensive, but the Synonyme line is kinder to your wallet. *Also see: St-Germain, Passy-Victor Hugo, St-Germain, Le Marais.*

24. Joseph - Fashionable Womenswear

277, rue Saint Honoré
01 53 45 83 30
M W

M° Concorde
Mon-Sat 10.30-19.30
€€

What started out as hairdresser Joseph Ettegdui selling knitwear by Miyake in his London-salon is today a huge success with stores in the UK and France. The winning formula is his clever take on sexy basics, giving them just the right amount of fashion edge. Besides his trademark knitwear and the suits and t-shirts, it's the trousers with their fabulous cuts that make the girls go wild . Nowadays you can only find his own label in the boutiques. At this flagship store designed by Christian Biecher you'll also find the menswear line. Downstairs you find Joe's, a good place to stop for a quick bite. *Also see: Étienne Marcel - Les Halles, Montaigne - Fbg St-Honoré, St-Germain, Passy - Victor Hugo*

25. Pallas - Handmade Bags

21, rue St-Roch
01 46 33 29 28
A

M° Tuileries
Mon 14-19, Tue-Fri 09-19
€€€

For years Elsa Zanetti has been making handbags for the couture houses. At the rue St-Roch boutique-cum-studio you'll find her own designs, ranging from classic box leather shoulder bags to small embroidered evening pouches. All the styles can be ordered in a selection of colours.

26. Cabane de Zucca - Japanese Designer

8, rue St-Roch   M° Tuileries
01 44 58 98 88   Mon-Sat 10.00-19.00
M W A   €€

Former assistant to Issey Miyake, Zucca creates workwear inspired basics such as jeans, t-shirts and jackets with a fashionable touch for men and women. For women he also does more trendy stuff in 2002 this means floaty fabrics with floral and ethnic prints in gipsy skirts, peasant blouses and hip slung belts. Colours are soft; khakis, blues and pinks. The Birkenstocks with different prints are fun.

27. Éric Bergère - French Designer Wear

16, rue de la Sourdière   M° Louvre-Rivoli
01 47 03 33 19   Mon-Sat 10.00-19.30
A W   €€€

Éric Bergère is a favourite among the urban chic crowd, and the Japanese are wild about his clothes. After working for Hermès and Lanvin he kicked off his own label in 1988. Shape is his strength, built on versatile cuts and a strong sense of proportion. He has his own personal style of effortless youthful-chic, drawing inspirations from the 1980s sportswear and working with a generous palette of colours, and a minimum of details as seen in bell-bottom trousers and slim-fitting jackets. The accessories are another strong feature here.

28. Espace Comme des Garçons - Scent

23, pl. d. Marché St Honoré   M° Pyramides
01 47 03 15 03   Mon-Sat 11.00-19.30
B   €€

This cool futurist boudoir designed by Rei Kawakubo herself, only sells Comme des Garçons' scents. No clutter and fuss, simply clean bright space and the perfumes and scented candles on display, almost like in an art gallery. A somewhat odd feature is the men's swimwear.

29. JC de Castelbajac - French Fashion/Lifestyle

31, pl. d. Marché St-Honoré M° Pyramides
01 42 60 41 57 Mon-Sat 10.30-19.00
A M O W €€

Jean-Charles de Castelbajac was one of the first designers to mix clothes with furniture and household items – the phenomenon we refer to today as a concept-store. His clothes, reflecting his wacky sense of humour, have a unique style pairing bold pop art inspired prints with simple "un-cut" cuts and fabric fabrics. The store is full of kitschy small items, toys, special magazines and cool accessories from Bernhard Wilhelm and Jeremy Scott among others.

30. Philippe Model - Couture Millinery

33, pl. d. Marché St-Honoré M° Tuileries
01 42 96 89 02 Tue-Fri 10.00-19.00,
  Sat 11.00-19.00
A €€€

Once the hatter of the catwalks, Model is now society's first choice when it comes to hats for special occasions. His creations are extravagant with big feathers, fruits, flowers and other things you wouldn't expect to see on a hat. He also offers more discreet wedding and beachy hats if you want to play safe. Worth checking out are the shoes that have a personal style. Bridal shoes can also be found here.

31. Corinne Cobson - Parisian Funky Fashion

6, rue du Marché St-Honoré M° Tuileries
01 42 60 48 64 Mon 14.30-19.30,
  Tue-Sat 10.30-19.30
A B W €€

A young, funky fashion look that mixes soft romantic items with more rock n' roll edges - Cobson matches a print T-shirt with a prim floral skirt for example. Black is a favourite colour as are silky fabrics. If you want more Cobson, she also has her own beauty line and makes perfume as well as scented candles. *Also at: 1, rue Jacob.*

32. Zadig & Voltaire - Urban Trendy Womenswear

9, rue 29 Juillet	M° Tuileries
01 42 92 00 80	Mon 13-19.30,
	Tue-Sat 10.30-19.30
A W	€€

Young, urban and upbeat, Zadig et Voltaire's own label has great jumpers, coats and bags in smart fabric combinations of leather, nylon, suede etc. for the fashion-conscious. The boutique on rue 29 Juillet also sells other labels such as Helmut Lang Jeans, Philosophy by Ferretti and Jean Colonna amongst others. *Also at: 36, rue de Sévigné, stock (Le Marais), 15, rue du Jour (Étienne Marcel - Les Halles), 12 rue Sainte Croix de la Bretonnerie, 1-3, rue du Vieux Colombier (St-Germain), 16 bis, rue de Passy (Passy - Victor Hugo).*

33. Claude Litz - Exclusive Furs

12, rue de Castiglione	M° Tuileries
01 42 61 44 62	Mon-Sat 11.00-19.30
A W	€€€

If you're in a "fur things first" mood then head straight to Claude Litz, famous for his expensive coats and jackets in fox, rabbit, mink or leopard skins. And with that new fur in your hand a matching handbag will make no difference to your VISA account, so why not snatch one up from Litz own collection, Dolce & Gabbana, or Versace.

34. Annick Goutal - Perfume House

14, rue de Castiglione	M° Tuileries
01 46 33 03 15	Mon-Sat 10.00-19.00
B	€€€

You can't get enough of wonderful perfumes, can you? Favoured by celebs around the world, the Annick Goutal perfumes are floral and subtle. Among the most favoured are fresh Eau d'Hadrien and sensual Passion. New is Le Chèvrefeuille, French for honeysuckle, a single-flower fragrance. Besides the perfumes you also find eau de toilette, soap, body lotion and scented candles. A perfect place for gift-buying.

35. Rodolphe Menudier - Fashionable Women's Shoes

14, rue de Castiglione   M° Tuileries
01 42 60 86 27   Mon 11.00-19.30,
                                   Tue-Sat 10.30-19.30
A M W   €€€

This ultra-chic boutique, designed by Christophe Pillet, is the perfect playground for shoe fetishists. Menudier has designed shoes for major fashion houses such as Balenciaga, Chloé and Dior. He first launched is own collection in 1994, and in 1996 he added a men's line. The style is always self-assured and sexy – pumps, sling-backs and boots all come with glamorous high heels. To add that final touch to your posh shopping experience, you walk away with your new treasures in a black satin bag.

36. Bleu Comme Bleu Vendôme - Spa and Beauty Centre

2, rue de Castiglione   M° Tuileries
01 58 62 54 54   Mon-Sat 9.30-19.00
A B M W   €€€

This huge complex is devoted entirely to feeling good. With its large spa and beauty centre, it's a good place for serious pampering. Clothes don't play a big part here, but you'll find a well-selected collection from labels such as Jérôme L'Huillier, Marcel Marongiu, and shoes by Christian Lacroix. In the café you can pick up light Italian dishes.

37. Giorgio Armani - Italian Designer Wear

6, place Vendôme   M° Opéra
01 42 61 55 09   Mon 11-19, Tue-Sat 10.30-19
A M W   €€€

The master of assured relaxed tailoring, Giorgio Armani's style was groundbreaking in the 1980s. A forerunner of the minimalist look, he took the stiffness out of men's suits and also transformed them into a work uniform for women. Today an Armani suit is still a sign of taste, with elegant clean lines and the minimum of detailing. The womenswear is feminine with soft fabrics and silhouettes, but often it still has a masculine quality to it. Over the seasons the collections haven't changed much, but there is a wider choice of colours now, not just the original neutrals. At this store you get the top Giorgio Armani label. *Also see Armani Collezioni (Montaigne Fbg-St Honoré) and Emporio Armani (St-Germain)*

38. Emporio Armani - Armani's diffusion line

25, place Vendôme   M° Opéra
01 42 61 02 34   Mon-Sat 10.00-19.00
A M W   €€

For details see St-Germain.

39. Charvet - Classic Men's Tailoring

28, place Vendôme   M° Opéra
01 42 60 30 70   Mon-Sat 10.00-18.45
M   €€€

In the world of fashion things come and go, but one thing stays put. Founded in 1838, the institution for Parisian male sartorial style, Charvet, still delivers brilliant woven silk ties and impeccably cut quality shirts. But forget browsing, here you shop like in the old days, with a salesperson showing you the goods. There is a multitude of fabrics and colours to choose from (ties starts at €60) and the made-to-measure studio is on the second floor. Here prices start at € 200 for a shirt. Allow one month for delivery.

40. Maria Luisa - Cutting-edge Womenswear

2, rue Cambon   M° Concorde
01 47 03 96 15   Mon-Sat 10.30-19.00
A W   €€€

With her impeccable taste and connoisseur eye, Maria Luisa Poumaillou's multi-label store is the Parisian point of reference for design creations. She mixes the hottest of the established elite such as John Galliano, Clements Riberio, Costume National and Martin Margiela with talented young designers like Oliver Theyskens and Veronique Leroy. She was one of the first Paris stockist of Helmut Lang and Ann Demeulemeester. Check out the rest of her empire that is spread here at rue Cambon/Mont Thabor.

41. Maria Luisa Accessories - Designer Accessories

4, rue Cambon   M° Concorde
01 47 03 48 08   Mon-Sat 10.30-19.00
A W   €€€

This Maria Luisa shop is a must on a serious shoe shopping tour with goodies from Manolo Blahnik, Lulu Guiness and Roberto di Camerino. And if you can't get enough of those Manolo mules - good news, Maria Luisa has opened a new boutique selling only Manolos just around the corner at 36, rue Mont Thabor.

42. Costume National - Italian Designer Wear

5, rue Cambon   M° Madeleine
01 47 03 02 02   Mon-Sat 10.00-19.00
M W   €€€

Eventually the so sought-after Italian brand Costume National opens in Paris. The brand of the former Yohji Yamamoto designer Ennio Capasa has been a favorite among fashion professionals since its start back in the late 80s. His style is characterized by close-fitting silhouettes with influences from streetwear as well as the clean cuts of Japanese design. Capasa favour fabrics before details which is very well shown in both the men and womens line.

43. Tiki Tirawa – Sophisticated Knitwear

10, rue Cambon   M° Madeleine
01 42 96 97 11   Mon-Sat 11.00-19.00
W   €€

For details see St-Germain.

44. Apostrophe - Elegant French Fashion

23, rue Cambon   M° Concorde
01 42 61 30 81   Mon-Sat 10.00-19.00
W   €€

For details see Montaigne - Fbg St-Honoré

45. Chanel - French Designer Wear

29-31, rue Cambon   M° Madeleine
01 42 86 28 00   Mon-Fri 09.30-18.30
                                 Sat 10.00-18.30
A B M W   €€€

It was here in 1910 at 21, rue Cambon that Gabrielle Chanel started
what would forever change the way women dress. With her designs
inspired by men's clothing especially the uniforms, she took women's
fashion to a new level of comfort and low-key elegance. The hall-
marks of her style - the suit, the gilt chain handbag, the two-tone
shoe and the jewellery are still the timeless essences that the collections by Karl Lagerfeld are built around. His clever takes on the classics no doubts keep the fashion pack coming back for more. This
is the largest store with a huge selection of ready-to-wear clothes,
accessories, perfume, make-up and costume jewellery. *Also at: 42,
avenue Montaigne; 25, rue Royal (shoes) (Montaigne - Fbg St-Honoré).*

46. Fifi Chachnil - Flirty Lingerie

26, rue Cambon   M° Concorde
01 42 60 38 86   Mon-Sat 11.00-19.00
L W   €€€

The world of Fifi Chachnil is all about full-blown opulence in the
ultra-kitsch sense. "Nothing horrifies me more than minimalism" as
Delphine Véron, the woman behind the label puts it. Her signature
Lolita-look comes in the shape of exquisite baby-doll goodies with all
the frills, lace and pretty pastels a girl could possibly want. The styles
are built to lift your assets as well as your spirit whether you go for the
flirty dresses or the pretty negligées in this boudoir-styled boutique.

47. Maria Luisa Homme - Cutting-edge Menswear

19 bis, rue du Mont Thabor   M° Concorde
01 42 60 89 83   Mon-Sat 10.30-19.00
M   €€€

Luckily for all fashion-conscious guys, Maria Luisa expanded into menswear in 1999. With the same winning formula she juxtaposes the work of classic designers with younger talents, be it Comme des Garçons, Alexander McQueen, Helmut Lang, Thomas Maier or John Smedley.

48. Maria Luisa Mixte - Casual Designer Wear

38, rue du Mont Thabor   M° Concorde
01 42 96 47 81   Mon-Sat 10.30-19.00
M W   €€

The fourth Maria Luisa venue, Mixte, provides young, relaxed fashion for both sexes. With unrivalled service on hand you can pick out your favourite Zoomp, Earl Jean or Helmut Lang jeans. Or why not go for up-and-coming Gaspard Yurkievich.

49. D&G - Dolce & Gabbana's Diffusion Line

244, rue de Rivoli   M° Concorde
01 42 86 00 44   Mon-Sat 10.00-19.30
A M W   €€

Dolce & Gabbana's younger tongue-in-cheek sibling really loves to party. The less expensive line is a huge hit with girls and guys that want the labels on the outside rather than the inside. For that perfect pool party outfit snap up animal and big flower prints and beachwear with the right glam attitude. Or go for gold, there's plenty of it. Accessories continue the theme with the same bold statements and logo overload.

50. Junko Shimada - Japanese Designer Wear

13, rue Saint-Florentin   M° Concorde
01 42 60 84   Mon-Sat 10.00-19.00
A M W   €€€

In a boutique that changes its decor every season to match the collections, French-Japanese designer Shimada shows clothes for the fashionista with a strong personal style who wants to make a mark. The look is colourful with slinky dresses, deluxe track pants and harem trousers in shimmering fabrics like lame, leather, flower prints and mohair knits. Cuts and drapery have a glamorous seventies and eighties flavour.

51. Junk by Junko Shimada - Girlish Fashion

13, rue St Florentin   M° Concorde
 01 42 60 94 12   Mon-Sat 10.00-19.00
A M W   €€

Junko Shimada's younger sister is for the girlie in you. It's pink, ruffles and Hello Kitty en masse. Slim-cut separates, coats and suits still have an edgy flavour to them. Accessories include plastic bags with loud statements printed on them.

52. Nina Gill - Couture Accessories

17, rue Saint-Florentine   M° Madeleine
01 42 86 04 29   Mon 14-19
                                     Tue-Sat 10-12.30,13.30-19
A   €€€

If you are looking for handmade evening bags with exquisite detailing in a feminine, romantic but no-frills style, look no further. Nina Gill and her family have been doing embroidery for all of the famous couture houses for over 40 years. It's their own line that's on display here in soft fifties colours with a varying degree of pearls, stones and spangles. As well as the bags there are also shawls, scarves and a few elegant tops.

51. Victoire - Chic Womenswear

4, rue Duphot   M° Madeleine
01 55 35 95 05   Mon-Sat 10.00-19.00
W   €€

For details see Étienne Marcel - Les Halles.

Étienne Marcel - Les Halles

Over the last couple of years the fashion scene in the 2nd arrondisement has experienced something of a second gold rush.

Today it's the best place to go in Paris if you want anything from young, trendy fashion from the high-street and big denim labels to sports- and streetwear.

The second arrondisment is lively, with the bustling main street, rue Étienne Marcel, as the artery of the area. It's a very commercial district with shops, restaurants, and cafés stretching along the main streets. Fashion-wise rue Étienne Marcel has undergone a transformation since the late 90s. Today it simmers with activity, and this is the place if you're looking for young, trendy looks of the season. Big denim labels such as Girbaud, Replay, and Diesel all have their huge flashy flagships here.

There is also an array of mid-priced labels here. You can pick up the season's must-haves from Paul & Joe, Bill Tornade, and Sylvia Rielle amongst others. For cutting-edge fashion, there is Kokon To Zai. And for more designer labels check out the two Kabuki shops and French designer Barbara Bui.

Strictly speaking, everything on the north side of rue Étienne Marcel is in the second arrondisement and everything on the south side is in the first. But of course it's much more convenient to shop along rue Étienne Marcel as a whole. That's why you'll find both sides of the street in this chapter, as well as Les Halles, which also belongs to the first arrondissement.

Les Halles today is a bit shabby and in the shopping mall, Forum des Halles, it's all about high-street and teenage fashion. If you're there, you can always pop into the Espace des Createurs, which displays fashion from different young designers. Frankly the only other reason for fashion-hunters to seek this area out, is for trainers and streetwear that you'll find in the small streets between Les Halles and rue Rivoli. Together with rue Étienne Marcel and rue d'Argout this area has actually become something of a streetwear centre in Paris. If you continue south, you'll end up at rue Rivoli where you find a bunch of high-street chains like Zara and H&M.

Eating and drinking

Bon 2
2, rue 4-Septembre
01 44 55 51 55

After the restobar Bon success in Passy (16th), Philippe Starck has rolled out the sequel.

Café Étienne Marcel
34, rue Étienne Marcel
01 45 08 01 03

The latest venue by the Costes brothers has no sign or logo on the outside. Enter, and you'll find a café in a futuristic home style.

Barbara Bui Café
27, rue Étienne Marcel
01 45 08 04 04

A pleasant stop for lunch or a snack.

Somo
168, rue Montmartre
01 40 13 08 08

This new bar and restaurant offers an exiting kitchen that draws inspiration from every part of the world.

Grand Colbert
2, rue Vivienne
01 42 86 87 88

This classic 19th century brasserie is still going strong. Newly renowated with beautiful murals.

Zen
18, rue du Louvre
01 42 86 95 05
Don't let the anonymous facade fool you, enter and you'll get superb sushi.

L'Atelier Berger
49, rue Berger
01 40 28 00 00
www.atelierberger.com
An innovative and personal kitchen is what chief Jean Christiansen delivers at this friendly mid-priced venue.

Staying

Hôtel de Victoires Opéra
56 rue Montorgueil
01 42 36 41 08,
www.victoiresopera.com

A small but inspiring hotel with beautifully decorated rooms in dark tones. The location, in the middle of the bustling pedestrian street Montorgueil, a stone's throw from Rue Étienne Marcel, is terrific. Double rooms start at € 213.

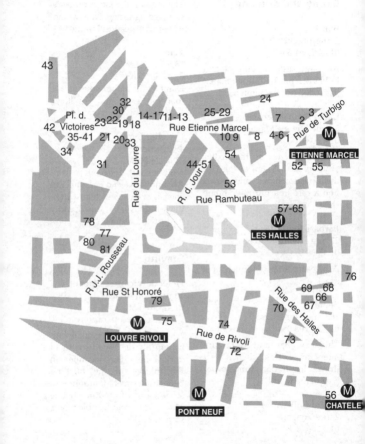

Rue de Turbigo
1. Scooter
2. Alain Tondowski
3. Et Vous Stock

Rue Étienne Marcel
4. Kabuki Homme
5. Barbara Bui
6. Kabuki Femme
7. Marc Le Bihan
8. Planisphere
9. Diesel
10. Ron Orb
11. E-Play
12. Replay
13. Marithé Francois Girbaud
14. Silvia Rielle
15. Gas
16. Joseph
17. Bill Tornade
18. Raw Essentials
19. Paul & Joe
20. Yohji Yamamoto
21. Energie/Miss Sixty
22. Bon Point
23. Cerruti Jeans

Rue Tiquetonne
24. Kokon To Zai
25. Maria Mercié
26. Anthony Peto
27. Lollipops
28. Patrick Cox
29. Kiliwatch

Rue d'Argout
30. Geda E-pure
30. Le Shop

Rue Hérold
31. Wowo

Rue du Louvre
32. Ventilo
33. Y´s

Rue la Vrillière
34. Adolfo Dominguez

Place des Victoires
35. Apostrophe
36. Kenzo
37. Cacharel
38. Thierry Mugler
39. Formes
40. Victoire
41. Plein Sud

Rue des Petit Pères
42. Michel Perry

Rue Vivienne
43. Galerie Gaultier

Rue du Jour
44. Diapositive
45. Pom d'Api
46. Zadig et Voltaire
47. Comptoir Des Cottoniers
48. Agnès B
49. Toi du Monde
50. Accessoire Jean-Paul Barriol
51. La Drouguerie

Rue Mondétour
52. Free Lance

Rue Montmartre
53. Claudie Perlot
54. Mokuba

Rue Pierre Lescot
55. Mosquitos

Rue Saint Denis
56. Du Pareil au Même

Forum des Halles
57. Sephora
58. Lollipops
59. Diesel
60. H&M
61. Muji
62. Zara
63. Mango
64. Espace Créateurs
65. Xuly-Bet

Rue Saint Opportune
66. Eight
67. Le Vestibule

Rue de la Ferronneie
68. Remixx
69. Lady Soul

Rue des Halles
70. Upla
71. The Village

Rue de Rivoli
72. Etam
73. H&M
74. Zara
75. Adidas Mégastore

Boulevard Sebastopol
76. Puma Store

Rue du Colonel Driant
77. Victoire

Rue Croix des Petis Champs
78. Robert Clergerie

Rue Saint Honoré Village
79. Tsun Do

Passage Vero-Dodat
80. By Terry

Rue Jean-Jacques Rousseau
81. Christian Louboutin

1. Scooter - Trend Jewellery

10, rue de Turbigo   M° Étienne Marcel
01 45 08 50 54   Mon-Fri 10-19
                                  Sat 11-19
A   €

Scooter has been popular for years with its kitschy designs, the sort that the teenage magazines are full of. It's the kind of jewellery that can make or break your outfit. They also do colourful handbags in different shapes and sizes. *Also at: 19, rue Dragon (St-Germain).*

2. Alain Tondowski - Designer Footwear

13, rue de Turbigo   M° Étienne Marcel
01 42 36 44 34   Mon-Sat 10.30-19.30
W   €€€

Alain Tondowski's ultra-cool boutique is a heaven for every shoe-aholic. Architect Eric Michaux's design is a sexy take on the 1970s interior style, a perfect match with Tondowski's killer stilettos. If you prefer more down-to earth footwear, this former Dior and Stephane Kélian team-mate can play that tune as well.

3. Et Vous - Contemporary Men and Womenswear

17, rue de Turbigo   M° Étienne Marcel
01 40 13 04 12   Mon-Sat 13.00-19.00
M W   €

This is Et Vous stock shop. For details see Le Marais.

4. Kabuki Homme - International Designer Wear

21, rue Étienne Marcel   M° Étienne Marcel
01 42 33 13 44   Mon-Sat 10.30-19.30
A M W   €€€

This is for young label-junkie guys. On the second floor you'll find cool suits, shirts and trousers from international designers like Helmut Lang, Miu-Miu and Costume National. For a more relaxed

look you'll find Prada Sport and Helmut Lang jeans. A small section
is devoted to casual women's clothes from Prada Sport. On the first
floor it's all about shoes, bags and other accessories.

5. Barbara Bui - Trendy Womenswear

23, rue Étienne Marcel   M° Étienne Marcel
01 40 26 43 65   Mon-Sat 10.30-19.30
W   €€

For further details see Montaigne - Fbg St Honoré

6. Kabuki Femme - International Designer Wear

25, rue Étienne Marcel   M° Étienne Marcel
01 42 33 55 65   Mon-Sat 10.30-19.30
A W   €€€

Owner William Halimi (husband of designer Barbara Bui) draws an
extremely fashion-conscious crowd to his multi-label Mecca. The
selection includes the hottest international designers, such as Balenciaga, Chloé, Costume National, Martine Sitbon and Helmut Lang.
The wide range of handbags and sunglasses includes names like
Prada, Fendi and Miu-Miu. For shoes pick up the seasons must-
haves from Marc Jacobs, Costume National and Sergio Rossi.

7. Marc Le Bihan - Designer Eyewear

22, rue Étienne Marcel   M° Étienne Marcel
01 42 36 22 32   Mon- 13-19.30,
                                Tues-Sat 10.30-19.30
A   €€€

If you're looking for eyewear that will fit your super-cool look this
is a must. You'll find a selection of all the designer labels that count
Dior, Gucci, Marc Jacobs, Matsuda, Fendi or YSL by Tom Ford. If
you're not into big designer logo sunglasses, but craves for indivi-
duality instead, go for Christian Roth's sleek futuristic models, gua-
ranteed logo-free. Lenny Kravitz is a big Roth fan.

8. Planisphere - Trendy Menswear

27, rue Étienne Marcel   M° Étienne Marcel
01 40 41 00 37   Mon-Sat 10.00-19.00
M   €€€

This boutique opened at the end of 2001 and the focus here is on fashionable menswear from different designers. You can pick up pieces from labels such as French Castelbajac, British Paul Smith and Italian Dolce et Gabbana's diffusion line D&G.

9. Diesel - Trendy Denims

35, rue Étienne Marcel   M° Étienne Marcel
01 42 21 37 55   Mon-Sat 10.00-19.00
M W   €€

Renzo Rossi still pleases the hip crowd - both young and old - with his unconventional denims; not bad after 20 years in the business. Besides the cool jeans, that come in an array of cuts and styles, the collections also includes shirts, dresses and tops in funky, playful styles. *Also at: Forum des Halles.*

10. Ron Orb - Urban Technowear

39, rue Étienne Marcel   M° Étienne Marcel
01 40 28 09 33   Mon-Sat 11.00-19.00
M W   €€

Ron Orb does androgynous clothes with a high-tech futuristic look. The cool urban pieces in synthetic fabrics are cut to fit the techno and streetwear generation.

11. E-Play - Streetwear

36, rue Étienne Marcel   M° Étienne Marcel
01 53 40 86 18   Mon-Sat 10.30-19.30
W M   €€

The area around rue Montorgueil and Étienne Marcel has become a hot spot for those into urban street-inspired outfits. E-play, the rebel sister of Replay, is one of the more edgy, with both modern and retro style elements. For a sexy ethnic feeling for her, pick up embroidered tees and glittery, twisted bra tops. For him, find cut and slash shirts with labels on the outside.

12. Replay - Trendy Denims

36, rue Étienne Marcel   M° Étienne Marcel
01 42 33 16 00   Mon-Sat 10.30-19.30
A M W   €€

Claudio Buziol's Replay store is strategically placed opposite former design partner, now rival, Renzo Rossi's Diesel store. And here, as at Diesel, denims in every shape, cut and wash are on display in an original interior made of stones, metals and lots of spotlights.

13. Marithé et Francois Girbaud - Denim and Leisurewear

38, rue Étienne Marcel   M° Étienne Marcel
01 53 40 74 20   Mon 12-19, Tue-Sat 10.00-19.00
M W   €€

Francois Girbaud and his partner Marithé Bachellerie, have built their mid-priced label's reputation around denim - the wardrobe of the working man, quite fitting for a company they founded in 1968, at the height of Paris' student-led political turmoil. The "jeanologists" as they call themselves, have since been relentless innovators in the areas of fabric, fit and finish. Their complex streetwear is laid back with a high comfort level. *Also at: 8, rue de Babylone; 7, rue du Cherche Midi, (St-Germain); 49, avenue Franklin D. Roosevelt (Montaigne-Fbg St-Honoré); 20, rue Mahler (denim line) (Le Marais).*

14. Sylvia Rielle - Fashionable Womenswear

42, rue Étienne Marcel   M° Étienne Marcel
01 42 36 26 00   Mon-Sat 11.00-19.30
W   €€

In the former Comme de Garçons boutique designer Sylvia Rielle, wife of Bill Tornade, has set up a new shop. It's more feminine in style than the Tornade womens collection, but still with detailing that gives the pieces more edge. Inspired by the big catwalk labels such as MiuMiu and Marni, with far more pleasant prices.

15. Gas – Ethnic-inspired Womens Clothes

44, rue Étienne Marcel   M° Étienne Marcel
01 42 33 36 04   Mon-Fri 10.30-19, Sat 11.00-19.00
A W   €€

Sexy sun-tanned ethnic is the look here. The pieces are made by different designers but the overall look is hippie-inspired. They stock Sigerson Morris shoes and their own accessories in a feminine style.

16. Joseph - Fashionable Womenswear

44, rue Étienne Marcel   M° Étienne Marcel
01 42 36 87 83   Mon-Sat 10.30-19.00
W   €€

For details see St-Honoré.

17. Bill Tornade - Fashionable Men and Womenswear

44, rue Étienne Marce   M° Étienne Marcel
01 42 33 66 47   Mon-Sat 11.00-19.30
M W   €€

Bill Tornade creates urban cool clothes for men and women. Deconstructed jeans, stretch dresses, and cleverly cut trousers - everything comes with a playful feeling for detailing and a sexy undertone. Reasonable prices. Tornade is also a favourite among the fashion-conscious for the children's line with avant-garde clothes for cool little ones. *Also at: 32, rue du Four (children's clothes) (St-Germain).*

18. Raw Essentials - Streetwear

46, rue Étienne Marcel   M° Bourse
01 42 21 44 33   Mon 11-19, Tue-Sat 10.30-19
M W   €€

Raw Essentials sells Dutch label G-Star. It's an urban workwear style, with a military flavour. Denim is the big thing with jackets, work trousers and overalls. Even though there are different styles for women, the look is androgynous.

19. Paul & Joe - Trendy Men and Womenswear

46 rue Étienne Marcel   M° Étienne Marcel
01 40 28 03 34   Mon-Sat 10.00-19.30
A W   €€

Want a young take on the season's trends at half the price of top designer labels? The place to go is Paul & Joe. French designer Sophie Albou's look is Parisian sexy and groovy. Her formula is to take retro-styled fabrics and cuts, and give them a modern twist. Rue Étienne Marcel only stocks womenswear. *Also at: 62, rue des Saints Peres, men's at 40, rue de Four (St-Germain).*

20. Yohji Yamamoto Pour Homme - Japanese Fashion

47, rue Étienne Marcel   M° Étienne Marcel
01 45 08 82 45   Mon 11.30-19.00
     Tue-Sat 10.30-19.00
M   €€€

Yohji Yamamoto's clothes for men are more relaxed, less poetic than his womenswear. He launched his first men's collection in 1984 and since then he has continued to push the boundaries. He has always dressed artsy, intellectual men. Lately he has been going for the tough-guy look with suits characterized by original details and fabrics. For more information see St-Germain.

21. Energie/Miss Sixty - Teenage Fashion

49 ,rue Étienne Marcel   M° Étienne Marcel
01 45 08 85 99   Mon-Sat 11.00-19.30
M W   €€

This red three-storey shop with tattooed young salesmen and twinkling floors is a teenager's heaven, selling the complete look as seen on MTV. The style is full of 1970s inspiration in denims and tight tops with nostalgic prints.

22. Bon Point - Children's Clothes

50, rue Étienne Marcel   M° Étienne Marcel
01 40 26 20 90   Mon-Sat 10.00-19.00
C   €€

Bon Point's children's clothes are very French meaning really pretty, almost prince and princess-like. These are not clothes for everyday, but rather for that special occasion when you don't think about practicality. In soft pastels and fine fabrics the clothes range from 0-8 years for boys and girls. They also do teenage and adult womenswear. The wonderful wool and cashmere blankets and shawls make the perfect gift – you don't have to worry about sizes. *There are branches in the 7th, 8th and 16th arrondissement (St-Germain, Montaigne - St-Honoré, Passy - Victor Hugo)*

23. Cerruti Jeans - Italian Casual Wear

52, rue Étienne Marcel   M° Étienne Marcel
01 53 00 92 61   Mon-Sat 10.00-19.00
M W   €€

Cerrutti's junior line is an urban casual affair. There is, of course, denim in relaxed and also more formal styles. For men the look is straight with button-down collars, sweaters and leather jackets. Upstairs there are young sporty day-to-evening skirts, trousers and blouses for women.

24. Kokon To Zai - Cutting-edge Designer Wear

48, rue Tiquetonne   M° Étienne Marcel
01 42 36 92 41   Mon-Sat 11.30-19.00
A M W   €€€

For every serious fashion shopper this boutique is a must. The store is small, but the one-off pieces and prêt-a-porter come from the hottest new talents. Find clothes by Marjan Pejoski (the brains behind the shop), Viktor & Rolf, Oscar Suleyman, Alexander Matthieu, Gaspard Yurkievich, Eley Kishimoto and Bernard Wilhelm. Accessories are equally stunning.

25. Maria Mercié - Stylish Hats

56, rue Tiquetonne	M° Étienne Marcel
01 40 26 60 68	Mon-Sat 11.00-19.00
A	€€

One of the modern milliner masters, Maria Mercié makes hats for women with attitude. The look is elegant and stylish, sometimes flamboyant. All hats are hand-made, and there is also a made-to-measure service. There are casual as well as more dressed-up styles. She also makes wonderful bridal hats. Prices start at €70. *Also at: 23, rue Saint Sulpice (St-Germain).*

26. Anthony Peto - Men's Hats

56, rue Tiquetonne	M° Étienne Marcel
01 40 26 60 68	Mon-Sat 11.00-19.00
A M	€€

British Anthony Peto, milliner Marie Mercié's husband, is for the man who loves hats. Stylish headware from panamas and fedoras to rasta berets and winter styles - it's all there. The shop also has a small range of ties and shirts from Vivienne Westwood and Paul Smith.

27. Lollipops - Fashionable Accessories

60, rue Tiquetonne	M° Étienne Marcel
01 42 33 15 72	Mon-Sat 11.00-19.30
A	€€

Look closely and you'll see that here, there is something for every one who wants trendy accessories without investing a small fortune. For the newly-launched line Lollipops Atelier, the designer Marjorie Mathieu, has made more elaborate and sophisticated products - using higher quality materials, more handwork and neater edges. *Also at: 40, rue Dragon (St-Germain), Forum des Halles (Étienne Marcel - Les Halles).*

28. Patrick Cox - Designer Shoes

62, rue Tiquetonne   M° Étienne Marcel
01 40 26 66 55   Mon-Sat 11.00-19.30
M W   €€€

The world went wild for his Wannabee loafers in the 1990s. Now, a couple of years later, the Canadian-born Cox still rocks with his cool, sometimes quirky designs for the fashion-conscious man or woman. His signature is the squared-off toe, and besides the more comfortable styles he also does dressier models like sexy high-heeled slingbacks and uncompromising stiletto boots with zips. *Also see: St-Germain*

29. Kiliwatch - Secondhand Clothes and Streetwear

64, rue Tiquetonne   M° Étienne Marcel
01 42 21 17 37   Mon 13-19, Tue-Fri 10.30-19
                                        Sat 10-19.30,
M O W   €

During the recent years craze for everything vintage, Kiliwatch's large secondhand store has pulled the hip young crowd, stylists and designers in search of inspiration. The styles change to fit fashion for the moment and they re-work some of the pieces accordingly. It is always a great place to find cool party clothes and it's prints must be a heaven for you to create your own outfits. They also sell mainstream streetwear and trendy magazines and books.

30. Geda. E-pure (corner at Le Shop) - Streetwear

3, rue d'Argout   M° Sentier
01 43 26 18 09   Mon13.00-17.00
                                        Tue-Sat 11.00-19.00
M W   €€

For details see Other Destinations.

30. Le Shop - Streetwear

3, rue d'Argout   M° Étienne Marcel
01 40 28 95 94   Mon 13-17,
                                         Tue-Sat 11-19

W M   €€

For the young street-savvy customer Le shop makes for a real shopping experience with it's multimedia displays and live DJs pumping
out the right grooves. The market-like stalls with individual outlets
sell clothes from labels such as Lady Soul, Freaks, Carhartt, Just Cow,
Sessün, and Komodo amongst others.

31. Wowo - Children's Clothes

4, rue Hérold   M° Sentier
01 53 40 84 80   Mon-Fri 11.30-19,
                                         Sat 14-19

C   €€

Designer Elizabeth Relin has her own personal style in children's wear. The
clothes for girls up to eight years come without the usual frills. Cute colourful clothes with tie-dye tops and trousers make for a hippie flavour.

32. Ventilo - French Classic Womenswear

27 bis, rue du Louvre   M° Étienne Marcel
01 44 76 82 95   Mon-Sat 10.30-19.30
A W O   €€

Take American sportswear and blend it with a hint of India, a spoon-ful
of American Indian and finally some British colonial spirit. Voilà, here we
have French Ventilo's design formula. Typical pieces are feminine shirts,
calf jodhpurs, floaty skirts, linen dresses and safari jackets. There's also a
home interior line in the same spirit. There is a bright salon du thé upstairs
at this branch. *Also at: 267, rue Saint Honoré (St-Honoré), 10, rue Francs Bourgeois (Le Marais), 59, rue Bonaparte (St-Germain), 49, avenue Victor Hugo and
96 avenue Paul Doumer (Passy - Victor Hugo).*

33. Y's - Yamamotos Diffusion Line

25, rue du Louvre	M° Louvre-Rivoli
01 42 21 42 93	Mon-Sat 10.30-19.00
W M	€€

For details see St-Germain.

34. Adolfo Dominguez - Spanish Men and Womenswear

4, rue la Vrillière	M° Palais-Royal M. du Louvre
01 42 60 09 94	Mon-Sat 10.00-19.00
A M W	€€

For details see Montaigne - Fbg St-Honoré.

35. Apostrophe - Elegant French Fashion

1 bis, place des Victoires	M° Bourse
01 40 41 91 94	Mon-Sat 10.00-19.00
W	€€

For information see Montaigne - St-Honoré.

36. Kenzo - French Designer Wear

3, place Victoires	M° Bourse
01 40 39 72 03	Mon-Sat 10.00-19.00
A M W	€€

For details see St-Germain.

37. Cacharel - French Designer Wear

5, place des Victoires	M° Bourse
01 42 33 29 88	Mon- Fri 10.30-19,
	Sat 10.30-19.30
A W	€€

For details see St-Germain.

38. Thierry Mugler - French Designer Wear

8, place des Victoires   M° Bourse
01 49 26 05 02   Mon-Sat 10.00-19.00
A M W   €€€

For details see St-Germain.

39. Formes - Maternity Wear

10, place des Victoires   M° Sentier
01 40 15 63 81   Mon-Sat 10.30-19.00
W   €€

A hit with pregnant women, Formes makes clothes that can take the style-conscious mum-to-be from the office to the cocktail party, with her fashion dignity intact. The quality clothes are sophisticated and modern with figure flattering silhouettes. *Also at: 12, Rue Sévigné (Le Marais), 5, rue Vieux Colombier (St-Germain), 41, rue de Passy (Passy - Victor Hugo).*

40. Victoire - Chic Men and Womenswear

10-12, place des Victoires   M° Bourse
01 42 60 96 21   Mon-Sat 10.00-19.00
W   €€

For women the flagship store offers a well-edited easy-to-wear mix of designer trends, such as Donna Karan, Marni and Philosophy. The other women's shops don't have the same trend-factor with a lot of safe mainstream chic in navy, stripes and casual pieces. The men's shops focus on their own label: bright coloured shirts for a casual Friday look are the best bet, and they come in a variety of unusual textures. *Also at: 4, rue Duphot , 10 rue Colonel Driant (men) (St-Honoré), 1, rue Madame, 15, rue du Vieux Colombier (men) (St-Germain), 16, rue de Passy (Passy - Victor Hugo).*

41. Plein Sud - Trendy Womenswear

14, place des Victoires   M° Bourse
01 42 36 75 02   Mon-Sat 11.00-19.00
W   €€

Moroccan designer Faycal Amor's label, Plein Sud attracts many women with its devastating sexy style. The Frenchified label is a huge success with trendy, technologically-edged collections that use innovative fabrics and body-conscious silhouettes. *Also at: 21, rue des Francs Bourgeois (Le Marais), 70 bis, rue Bonaparte (St-Germain), and 2, Avenue Montaigne (Montaigne - Fbg St Honoré).*

42. Michel Perry - Sexy Designer Shoes

4 bis, rue des Petit-Pères   M° Sentier
01 42 44 10 07   Mon-Sat 11.00-19.00
W   €€€

Michel Perry's is rated high by the fashionistas. His original designs are long and narrow – almost fetishistic - for women who have their own style. The heels, his magic weapon, are always sky-high and in lots of different shapes - stilettos or his signature thick rounded heel. Every season he comes up with brand new ones. This stylish boutique is the perfect setting for shoe excesses with it's draped orange and pink curtains à la boudoir. There's also a small but delicious collection of clothes by Chloé, Julian McDonald, Boyd and Mathilde.

43. Galerie Gaultier - French Couturier

6, rue Vivienne   M° Bourse
01 42 86 05 05   Mon, Sat 11-19, Tue-Fri 10.30-19.30
A M W   €€€

For details see the Other Destinations.

44. Diapositive - Fashionable Womenswear

12, rue du Jour   M° Les Halles
01 42 21 34 41   Mon 12.30-19, Tue-Sat 10.30-19
W   €

Diapositive is a good place to shop for inexpensive, wearable takes on the season's catwalk trends. The cuts are classic, and there is a grown-up feeling to the collections, as seen in the business suits and evening wear. *Also at: 42, rue du Four; 33, rue de Sèvres (St-Germain).*

45. Pom d' Api - Children's Shoes

13, rue du Jour   M° Les Halles
01 42 36 08 87   Mon-Sat 10.00-19.00
C   €€

If mum wears Free Lance, the kids can match with equally trendy shoes from Pom d'Api, also by the Rautureau family. The cool shoes are comfortable and there are styles for every occasion. Sizes go from 18 to 27.

46. Zadig & Voltaire - Urban Trendy Womenswear

15, rue du Jour   M° Les Halles
01 42 21 88 70   Tue-Sat 10.30-19.30, Mon 13-19.30
W   €€

For details see Saint Honoré.

47. Comptoir Des Cotonniers - Basics

29, rue du Jour   M° Les Halles
01 53 40 75 77   Mon-Sat 10.00-19.00
W   €

For details see St-Germain.

48. Agnès b. - French Casual Chic

2, 3, 6, 10, rue du Jour   M° Les Halles
01 45 08 56 56   Mon-Sat 10.00-19.00
A C M O W   €€

Since Agnès Troublé, the woman behind Agnès b., opened her first shop in 1975 her designs have been based on utilitarian clothing such as workmen's blue overalls and undershirts, paying little attention to fashion. It's this formula of casual chic that keeps her alive and kicking year after year. The neutral coloured high-quality wardrobe staples like crisp white cotton shirts, plain knitwear, t-shirts and pared-down tailoring appeal to a wide range of men and women of all ages and lifestyles. *Also see: St-Germain, Montaigne - Fbg St-Honoré, Other Destinations.*

49. Toi du Monde - Fashionable Womenswear

7, rue du Jour   M° Les Halles
01 40 13 09 32   Mon 13-19.30, Tue-Sat 10.30-19
W   €€

Created in 1988 by Athos Lanciotti, Toi du Monde offers up-to-date, urban style clothing for modern women looking for accessible creativity. Technically modern fabrics are the focus point of each collection of affordable, fashion-minded pieces. *Also at: 24, rue de Sévigné (Le Marais); 3, rue Montfaucon (St-Germain).*

50. Accessoire Jean-Paul Barriol - Modern Footwear

8, rue du Jour   M° Les Halles
01 40 26 19 84   Mon-Sat 11.00-19.00
A W   €€

For details see St-Germain.

51. La Drouguerie - Haberdashery

9-11, rue du Jour   M° Les Halles
01 45 08 93 27   Mon 14.00-18.45,
                                  Tue-Sat 10.30-18.45
O   €

This must be one of the best places in Paris to meet up-and-coming designer talents. Everything you need to give that haberdashery habit of yours a real bite is on display here. Stylish buttons, braiding, feathers and fringes, trimmings of every kind - this store is the best.

52. Free Lance - Fashion Footwear

22, rue Mondétour   M° Étienne Marcel
01 42 33 74 70   Mon-Fri 10-19, Sat 10-19.30
M W   €€

For details see St-Germain.

53. Claudie Pierlot – French Womenswear

1, rue Montmartre   M° Les Halles
01 42 21 38 38   Mon 13-19, Tue-Sat 11-19
W   €€

Claudie Pierlot epitomizes the classic French look, what a Parisian girl's wardrobe is made up of. The clothes are feminine, in a youthful, but not trendy way, with prints and colours that have a retro flavour to them. Next door at 3, rue Montmartre, Pierlot sells her more moderately priced second line, Mon Ami Pierlot, casual clothing and swimwear for holidays and weekends. *Also at: 23, rue du Vieux-Colombier (St-Germain).*

54. Mokuba - Haberdashery

18, rue Montmartre   M° Les Halles
01 40 13 81 41   Mon-Fri 09.30-18.30
O   €

Haberdashery-loving girls and boys watch this space. When it comes to ribbon retailing, Japanese Mokuba is world-class. There isn't a couture house worth it's name that doesn't come here regularly. There are more than 37,000 different kinds of ribbons, and they also stock lace, leather, faux fur and frogging.

55. Mosquitos - Funky Footwear

19, rue Pierre Lescot   M° Étienne Marcel
01 45 08 44 72   Mon-Sat 10.00-19.00
M W   €€

If you want up-to-date footwear but don't want to spend a fortune on it, Mosquitos could be worth a try. The look is young, clubby and colourful. The shoes are made in Spain, Italy and Portugal, so the prices are more affordable. *Also at: 25, rue du Four, 99, rue de Rennes (St-Germain).*

56. Du Pareil au Même - Children's Clothes

1, rue Saint Denis   M° Châtelet
01 42 36 07 57   Mon-Sat 10.00-19.00
A M W   €€

Fashion-conscious mums come here for cool and very reasonably priced kids wear. Colour, details and prints have a modern but distinctly French flavour. The designs do not reflect the trend-of-the-month that makes kids look like precocious MTV-popstars. Du Pareil Au Même Bébé has the same concept but is for babies. *Branches are scattered all over Paris for example 14, rue St Placide, 168, boulevard St Germain, 15-17 rue des Mathurins, 97 avenue Victor Hugo. Bébé stores can be found at 34, St Placide and 23, rue des Mathurins amongst others.*

57. Sephora - Beauty Megastore

Forum des Halles   M° Les Halles
01 40 13 72 25   Mon-Sat 10.00-19.30
B   €€

For details see the Montaigne-Fbg St-Honoré.

58. Lollipops - Fashionable Accessories

Forum des Halles   M° Les Halles
01 40 26 32 95   Mon-Sat 10.00-19.30
A   €€

For details see no 27 this chapter.

59. Diesel - Trendy Denims

Forum des Halles   M° Les Halles
01 40 26 73 85   Mon-Sat 10.00-19.30
M W   €€

For details see no 9 this chapter.

60. H&M - High-Street Fashion

Forum des Halles   M° Les Halles
01 55 34 79 99   Mon-Sat 10.00-19.30
A C M W   €

For details see no 73 this chapter.

61. Muji - Japanese Basics

Forum des Halles   M° Les Halles
01 44 88 56 56   Mon-Sat 10.00-19.00
A B M O W   €

For details see St-Germain.

62. Zara - Spanish High-Street Fashion

Forum des Halles   M° Les Halles
01 55 34 98 51   Mon-Sat 10.00-19.30
A M W   €

For details see no 74 this chapter.

63. Mango - High-Street Fashion

Forum des Halles   M° Les Halles
01 42 36 76 20   Mon-Sat 10.00-20.00
A W   €

Mango is another Spanish high-street fashion chain that has expanded its territory to every big European city. The winning weapon is their low-priced takes on every catwalk trend, as long as they suits the Mango girl who is young, slim and wants clothes with that sexy-babe-look. However, bargain of the day are the leather items. It doesn't get better than this anywhere else at these prices. *Also at: 3, place du 18 Juin 1940 (6th, not listed); 6, boulevard des Capucines (Opéra).*

64. Espace Créateurs - Young Designers

Forum des Halles   M° Les Halles
01 40 39 09 56   Mon-Sat 11.00-19.30
M W   €€

Espace Créateurs is the only reason for the fashionista to include Forum les Halles in a serious shopping tour. Spread over 1000 square metres in eight different boutiques, clothes by more than 50 designers are on display. As you would expect, there is a huge range of styles and looks. The unifying force is that it's all about young designers as Xuly-Bet, Erotokritos, Yao Souka, FuturWareLab, Yoshi Kondo, Chantal Jaillot among others.

65. Xuly-Bet - Funky Womenswear

5, Forum des Halles	M° Les Halles
01 42 33 47 50	Mon-Sat 11.00-19.30
W	€€

For details see Le Marais.

66. Eight - Trainers

5, rue Saint Opportune	M° Les Halles
01 40 26 87 09	Mon-Sat 11.00-19.30
M W	€€

For trendy trainers this shop is a good reference point, with labels such as Nike, Adidas, Reebok and Coq Sportif.

67. Le Vestibule - Trendy Clubwear

3, Place Saint Opportune	M° Les Halles
01 42 33 21 89	Mon-Sat 10.30-19.00
M W	€€

This multi-brand shop is definitly worth checking out if you're looking for cool clubwear. Labels include Dolce & Gabbana, Dirk Bikkemberg, Castelbajac, Cultura and Diesel StyleLab.

68. Remixx - Trainers

7, rue de la Ferronnerie	M° Châtelet
01 40 26 63 58	Mon-Sat 11.00-20.00
M W	€€

Remixx is all about trainers. There are more than 120 styles – ranging from utterly modern to retro - all carefully selected by the trio behind the store. Choose from Puma, Ecko, Wolverine, Adidas amongst others.

69. Lady Soul - Streetwear

31, rue de la Ferronnerie   M° Châtelet
01 40 28 05 59   Mon 14-19, Tue-Sat 11.15-19
W   €€

You know your label has street cred when a hip magazine offers you free advertising. That's what happened to cult label Lady Soul. Since 1994 the French duo Zina Kerachnoiu & Alexandre Guarneri have been making funky streetwear for girls. The inspiration comes from street fashion, music and underground art. The collections contain cool relaxed items such as hooded sweaters, baggy trousers, denim dresses and skirts. The palette includes dark blue, khaki, red and claret.

70. Upla – Lifestyle

17, rue des Halles   M° Châtelet
01 40 26 49 96   Mon-Sat 10.30-19.00
A B M W O   €€

In the spacious Upla stores Catherine Barade offers a variety of products with emphasis on natural living. Beauty products, fashion accessories, and of course own-brand collection of clothing-classics for men and women are on display here. *Also at: 5, rue St-Benoît.*

71. The Village - Streetwear

22, rue des Halles   M° Châtelet
01 40 39 09 06   Mon-Sat 11.00-19.30
M W   €€

The Village is a cool store with urban street style labels. Choose from Stüssy, Cultura, and Full Circle among others. Downstairs there's a collection of 1950s vintage clothing for all those fripe-freaks.

72. Etam - High-Street Womenswear

73, rue de Rivoli   M° Châtelet
01 44 76 73 73   Mon-Sat 10.00-19.00
C L W   €

In this former Samaritaine building the high-street womenswear label, Etam, has created an immense flagship store. Especially it's a good place for inexpensive lingerie. The selection is impressive and there are styles for all ages and sizes. Swimwear is also a good bet, with many trendy pieces. They also do sportswear, maternity, kid's and business clothes. Considering the prices the quality is acceptable, but don't expect the clothes to last for years. On the top-floor there is a bright, modern restaurant with nice views. *Also at: branches all over Paris.*

73. H&M - High-Street Fashion

120, rue de Rivoli   M° Châtelet
01 55 34 96 86   Mon-Sat 10.00-20.00
A B C M W   €

This Swedish chain has conquered the world with clothes that have this season's look at all-time-low prices. The most fashionable lines are "Clothes" with edgy takes on trends of the moment and "Divided", the young denim line. You can also find good basics and sportswear here. For men the best bet is leisure and young trendy stuff. Business suiting doesn't stand the test at these low prices. Kids clothes are up-to-date in an informal style. Considering the prices the quality is acceptable, but it fluctuates. *Also at: Forum des Halles, 135, rue de Rennes (St-Germain), 54, boulevard Haussmann, 107, rue St Lazare (Opéra), 53, rue de Passy (Passy - Victor Hugo).*

74. Zara - Spanish High-Street Fashion

128, rue de Rivoli   M° Châtelet
01 44 82 64 00   Mon-Sat 10.00-20.00
A C M W   €

All over Paris you find Zara, one of the best high-street fashion chains around. What this Spanish company excels in is inexpensive takes on the catwalk looks. Come here for that season's flavour that will give your wardrobe the look of the moment. But it's best to look for business clothes like suits (that goes for men and women) in other places. Basics such as shell tops and kid's simple but modern clothes are a good bet. *Also at: branches all over central Paris.*

75. Adidas Mégastore - Leisure and Sportswear

148, rue de Rivoli
01 42 60 34 83
M W

M° Louvre-Rivoli
Mon-Sat 10.00-19.30
€€

Glass panels, video monitors and computers to play around with, it's all here at this futuristic cyber-dome of sports gear. You will find clothes for every sport and of course they stock every kind of Adidias-trainer too.

76. Puma Store - Sportswear

22, boulevard Sebastopol
01 44 59 88 02
C M W

M° Châtelet
Mon-Sat 10.30-19.30
€€

After San Francisco, Moscow, Los Angeles and Tokyo, Puma's fifth concept-store opened in Paris 2001. Riding high on the retro sportswear trend, Puma has joined forces with Jil Sander. The result so far is a line of cool, old-school styled trainers. At the Sebastopol flagship store you will find everything for your sports and leisure wardrobe. Even your youngest family members can get the right sports gear here.

77. Victoire - Chic Menswear

10, rue du Colonel Driant
01 42 97 44 87
M

M° Palais-Royal M. du Louvre
Mon-Sat 10.00-19.00
€€

For details see 10-12 place des Victoires, this chapter.

78. Robert Clergerie - French Designer Shoes

46, rue Cr. des Petits Champs
01 42 61 49 24
M W

M° Palais-Royal M. du Louvre
Mon-Sat 10.00-19.00
€€

For details see St-Germain.

79. Tsun Do - Far East Fashion

91, rue St-Honoré, Village	M° Louvre-Rivoli
01 42 36 56 67	Mon-Sat 11.00-19.30
O W	€€

This is the first shop in Paris to sell creations by young Asian designers that reflect traditional Asian clothing. Intricate embroideries, fine silk and cashmere go with the style. You'll also find antique and modern furniture, and design objects from the Far East.

80. By Terry - Personalized Cosmetics

21, passage Vero-Dodat	M° Louvre-Rivoli
01 44 76 00 76	Mon-Sat 11.00-19.00
B	€€€

In this sleek modern shop Terry de Gunzburg, a former creative director for Yves Saint Laurent, and her team will create products especially for you (about €450). If you prefer the "ready-to-wear" collection, look for products such as the unique Colour Skin Enchancer. Whatever you choose, you can expect top quality ingredients. *Also at: 1, rue Jacob (St-Germain) A new shop will open in late 2002 at 10, avenue de Victor Hugo.*

81. Christian Louboutin - Designer Shoes

19, rue J-Jacques Rousseau	M° Les Halles
01 42 36 05 31	Mon-Sat 10.30-19.00
W	€€€

Famous shoemaker Christian Louboutin's trademark red soles can be seen on the world's glitterati and royals. The attraction is his seductive style may it be classic elegance or forbidden fantasy. But whatever degree of innovation, the styles are always truly beautiful and wearable. As Louboutin himself puts it " It's a cross between a weapon or a work tool and an objet d'art. *Also at: 38-40, rue Grenelle (St-Germain)*

3/4

Le Marais

The charming Le Marais is for the artsy and preferable wealthy fashion-seekers, wanting intellectual looks mixed with bohemian-chic styles.

With it's beautiful 17th century mansions, cobbled streets and small courtyards, Le Marais, that makes up the 3rd and the 4th arrondissements, has an idyllic and romantic atmosphere. The oldest square in Paris, the Place des Vosges, is also one of the most beautiful places, and fittingly Japanese designer Issey Miyake has his main shop here.

The streets are full of small boutiques, lively cafés and bars and the area has a lovely mix of people, with the old Jewish quarter as well as the gay community. Many artists, actors, filmmakers, and designers also live here, something that pretty much sets the tone for the style of fashion you find in the small personal boutiques in the main street; rue des Francs Bourgeois, and adjoining streets like rue des Rosiers and rue Mahler.

Miyake's high-tech clothes at A-POC and his other concept Pleats Please are both located here. Azzedine Ala a has his mansion on rue de Moussy. On rue des Rosiers you'll find the multi-label shop L'Éclaireur, which stocks almost all the international designers that count. If you're looking for something different from the Prada-this and Prada-that, this area is the perfect hunting ground for lesser known designers such as French José Levy, Australian Martin Grant, Japanese Tsumori Chisato, and Italian Paoula Frani. Recently the Diesel label, New York Industries, opened its first mono-label store on rue Pavée. For cheaper clothes, there is a bunch of shops like Et Vous, Antoine et Lili, Zadig et Voltaire, with prices a notch or two above the high-street chains.

If you want to do some Sunday shopping this is the best place to go, since it's the only area where some of the boutiques are open.

Eating and drinking

Georges
Centre Pompidou, 6th floor
01 44 78 85 47

Spectacular view, bustling atmosphere and fairly good food makes this Costes-brothers venue worth a visit. Also try their lunch on the terrace.

L'Ambroisie
9 place des Vosges
01 42 78 51 45

When you want to mix romance with the best gourmet cooking, this is the place. Just be sure you pick the perfect date, as the visit will definitely make it's mark on your wallet.

Le Hangar
12, impasse Berthaud
01 42 74 55 44

This venue draws those in the know with it's clever interpretations of the classical cuisine.

Les Philosophes
28, rue Vieille du Temple

A bustling café that attracts a mix of Jews, gays and fashion types.

La Charlotte en I'Ile
24, rue St-Louis-en-I'Ile
01 43 54 25 83

For delicous thés and superb dark chocolate this petite café is a winner.

Chez Omar
47, rue de Bretagne
01 42 72 36 26

A crowded bistro that serves Omar's splendid Couscous Royal and other North African dishes.

Staying

Hôtel Axial Beaubourg
11 rue du Temple
01 42 72 72 22

Newly redecorated, this mid-price hotel is among the latest on the Paris design hotel scene. Nice dark and soft-coloured rooms in a no-fuss style. A strategic position between Le Marais and Les Halles.

Jeu de Paume
54, rue St-Louis-en-I'Ile
01 43 26 14 18

Dating back to the 17th century this hotel situated on the island I'lle St-Louis has all the romance-factor you'll need. Expect to pay €150 for a double.

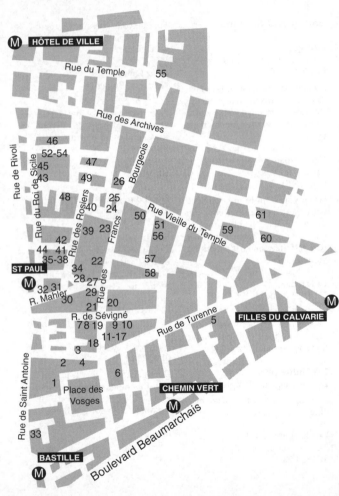

Place des Vosges
1. Issey Miyake

Rue de Turenne
2. Anna Kaszer
3. Fifi de Vem
4. Antik Batik
5. Georges Rech

Rue du Foin
6. Antik Batik Enfant

Rue Sévigné
7. Formes
8. Losco
9. Zadig et Voltaire (Stock)
10. La Licorne

Rue des Francs Bourgeois
11. Sequoia
12. Et Vous
13. Autour du Monde
14. Abou D'abi Bazar
15. Ventilo
16. Cécile et Jeanne
17. Anne Fontaine
18. Camper
19. Plein Sud
20. Jean-Claude Monderer
21. Mare
22. Comptoir Des Cotonniers
23. Barbara Bui
24. Muji
25. A-POC
26. Antoine et Lili

Rue Pavée
27. Regina Rubens
28. New York Industries

Rue Mahler
29. Paule Ka
29. Marithé et Francois Girbaud
30. L'Éclaireur Homme
31. Culotte
32. Anna Kaszer

Rue Saint Antoine
33. Comptoir Des Cotonniers

Rue des Rosiers
34. ICB
35. Paoula Frani
36. Pleats Please
37. L'Éclaireur
38. Tiziana Pavan
39. Martin Grant
40. Jack Henry

Rue F. Duval
41. Bethsabée
42. Le Clan des Chineurs

Rue du Roi de Sicile
43. Serge Amoruso
44. La Copine à Teddy Bear
45. Mamz'elle Swing

Rue de Moussy
46. Azzedine Ala a

Rue St-Croix de la Brettoniere
47. Zadig & Voltaire

Rue Vieille du Temple
48. Accessoire Jean-Paul Barriol
49. Selima Optique
50. FutureWare Lab
51. José Lévy à Paris

Rue Bourg-Tibourg
52. Jean-Baptiste Rautureau
53. Nim
54. Anatomica

Rue Rambeteau
55. Menkes

Rue Barbette
56. Tsumori Chisato

Rue Elzévyr
57. Nicole Cadine
58. Xuly-Bet

Rue du Perche
59. C. Charon

Rue de Poitou
60. Karine Dupont
61. L'Habilleur

1. Issey Miyake - Japanese Designer Wear

3, place des Vosges
01 48 87 01 86
M W

M° St-Paul
Mon-Sat 10.00-19.00
€€€

Issey Miyake is part of the Japanese fashion elite that conquered Paris in the 1980s. Hugely influential, he has always been one step ahead with his highly innovative clothes. The outfits, characterized by vibrant colours, haute-couture details and new shapes, often involving wrapping and layering fabric, have always been worn by intellectuals and artsy types. Today Miyake is concentrating on the Pleats Please and A-POC labels and Naoki Takizawa handles the mainline, bringing forward original and comfortable pieces with a romantic feel for women and clear-cut menswear. In this beautiful store you find both the men and womenswear.

2. Anna Kaszer - Contemporary Womenswear

16, rue de Turenne
01 42 71 51 10
W

M° St-Paul
Mon-Sat 11-19.30 Sun 14-19
€€

For details see no 32 this chapter.

3. Fifi de Vem - Children's Clothes

17, rue de Turenne
01 44 61 03 75

M° St-Paul
Mon-Sat 10.30.19.30
Sun 14.30-19.30

C

€€

For fashion-conscious mums and dads who want their little ones to dress accordingly, Fifi de Vem can be of great assistance. To match daddy's Dries there is a bunch of Belgian designers, as well as Baby Dior and La Perla to mix things up a little. The style is cool streetwear and the baby will be hippest on the block that's for sure.

4. Antik Batik - Bohemian Chic Men and Womenswear

18, rue de Turenne
01 44 78 02 00

M° St-Paul
Tue-Sat 11-19,
Mon 14-19

A M W

€€

Fashion's on-going craze for all things bohemian and ethnic continues and if that's what you are into, Antik Batik is one of Paris' hot spots. Owners Gabriella Cortese and Christophe Sauvat's take on 1970s hippie chic comes in the form of square-necked peasant blouses, patchwork chiffon dresses, and high-collar Victorian tops. The label is also becoming famous for it's antique-looking bags of embroidered velvet. Good value for money. *Also at: 8, rue du Foin (this chapter) (children's clothes); 38, rue de Vaugirad (St-Germain), .*

5. Georges Rech - French Chic

58, rue Turenne
01 42 77 12 60
M W

M° St-Paul
Mon-Sat 10.00-19.00
€€€

For details see Montaigne - St-Honoré.

6. Antik Batik Enfant - Children's Clothes

8, rue du Foin	M° Chemin Vert
01 40 29 49 93	Tue-Sat 11-13, 14-19
C	€€

For details see no 4 this chapter.

7. Formes - Maternity Wear

14, rue Sévigné	M° St Paul
01 42 74 26 76	Mon-Sat 10.30-19.00
W	€€

For details see Étienne Marcel - Les Halles.

8. Losco - Leather Accessories

20, rue Sévigné	M° St-Paul
01 48 04 39 93	Mon 14-19, Tue-Sat 11-13, 14-19
A	€€

A place worth popping into if you are after artisan belts and other leather accessories but don't want to go for expensive designer labels, or mass-produced chain labels. The style is down-to-earth, with cowboy and ethnic influences. *Also at: 5, rue de Sèvres (St-Germain).*

9. Zadig & Voltaire stock - Urban Trendy Womenswear

36, rue de Sévigné	M° St-Paul
01 42 77 47 77	Daily 14.00-19.30
W	€

This is Zadig & Voltaire's sale shop. For details see St-Honoré.

10. La Licorne - Costume Jewellery

38, rue de Sèvigné	M° St-Paul
01 48 87 84 43	Mon-Sat 14.30-18.30
A	€€

This is a treasure trove of costume jewellery from the 1920s and onwards. You'll have to have a little patience to sift through the knick-knacks, but you'll find great jade, pearl and tortoiseshell pieces. There's also a repair service.

11. Sequoia - Trendy Accessories

6, rue des Francs Bourgeois   M° St-Paul
01 48 04 78 28   Mon-Sat 10.00-19.00
A   €€

For details see St-Germain.

12. Et Vous - Fashionable Men and Womenswear

6, rue des Francs Bourgeois   M° St-Paul
01 42 71 75 11   Mon-Sat 10.30-19.00
M W   €€

Whatever trends the new season dictates, you can be sure to find a take on them in Koji Tatsuno's Et Vous collections. The pieces are always well-made, reasonably priced and with exactly the right amount of trend factor to suit a large crowd of the fashion-conscious. There are always fine basic items such as trousers, knits and coats. *Also at: 17, rue de Turbigo (Étienne Marcel - Les Halles); 46, rue du Four; 62, rue Rennes (menswear) (St-Germain); 72, rue de Passy (Passy-Victor Hugo).*

13. Autour du Monde - Casual Wear

8, rue des Francs Bourgeois   M° Hôtel-de-Ville
01 42 77 06 08   Mon 11-19.30,
    Tue-Sat 10.30-19.30, Sun 13-19
A M O W   €€

For details see St-Germain.

14. Abou D'abi Bazar - Fashionable Womenswear

10, rue des Francs Bourgeois   M° St-Paul
01 42 77 96 98   Mon 14-19,
                               Tue-Sat 10.30-19, Sun 14-19
W   €€

A multi-label store with affordable items from fashion-aware labels, such as Tara Jarmon, Ange, Paul & Joe and Les Petits. You also find Isabel Marant's streetwear.

15. Ventilo - French Classic Womenswear

10, rue des Francs Bourgeois   M° St-Paul
01 40 27 05 58   Mon-Sat 10.30-19.30
W   €€

For details see Étienne Marcel - Les Halles.

16. Cécile et Jeanne - Jewellery

12, rue des Francs Bourgeois   M° St-Paul
01 44 61 00 99   Mon-Sat 11.00-20.00
A   €€

For details see St-Honoré.

17. Anne Fontaine – White shirts for Women

12, rue des Francs Bourgeois   M° St-Paul
01 40 27 05 58   Mon-Sat 10.30-19.00
W   €€

For further details see St-Germain.

18. Camper - Casual Footwear

9, rue des Francs Bourgeois   M° Hôtel-de-Ville
01 48 87 09 09   Mon-Sat 10.00-19.00
M W   €€

For details see Montaigne - Fbg St-Honoré.

19. Plein Sud - Trendy Womenswear

21, rue des Francs Bourgeois   M° St-Paul
01 42 72 10 60   Mon-Sat 11-19, Sun 14-19
W   €€

For details see Étienne Marcel - Les Halles.

20. Jean-Claude Monderer - Contemporary Footwear

22, rue des Francs Bourgeois   M° St-Paul
01 48 04 51 41   Mon 10.30-19,
                                 Tue-Sat 10-19, Sun 14-19
M W   €€

A good place to find mid-priced footwear from labels such as
Camper, Clark's, Polo Sport and Kenzo. Their own line has a slightly
higher vamp-factor with pointy high-heels. *Also at: 2, carrefour de la
Croix-Rouge (St-Germain).*

21. Mare - Italian Fashionable Shoes

23, rue des Francs Bourgeois   M° St-Paul
01 48 04 74 63   Tue-Sat 11-19.30
                                 Mon 14-19
M W   €€

Italian shoe designer Nelle Nembro usually gets it right trendwise.
Whatever the season's look, you will find it here. There are two different lines: Mare is the sportier one, while the Nelle Nembro line fol-
lows the Italian tradition of sleek feminine footwear. *Also at: 4, rue du
Cherche-Midi (St-Germain).*

22. Comptoir Des Cotonniers – Basics

33, rue des Francs Bourgeois   M° St-Paul
01 42 76 95 33   Mon-Sat 10.00-19.00
W   €

For details see St-Germain.

23. Barbara Bui - Trendy Womenswear

43, rue des Francs Bourgeois   M° St-Paul
01 53 01 88 05   Mon 14-19, Tue-Sat 11-19
A W   €€

For further details see Montaigne-Fbg St-Honoré.

24. Muji - Japanese Basics

47, rue des Francs Bourgeois   M° Hôtel-de-Ville
01 49 96 41 41   Mon-Sat 10.00-19.00
B M O W   €

For details see St-Germain.

25. A-POC - Issey Miyake Customized Clothes

47, rue des Francs-Bourgeois   M° St-Paul
01 44 54 07 05   Tue-Sat 10.30-19.30
M W   €€

Issey Miyake continues to push the boundaries with his latest venture, A-POC, short for "A Piece of Cloth". It's a conceptual approach to how clothes are manufactured. Skirts, trousers, dresses and even underwear are cut of from great rolls of fabric according to your specification. In the age of customized fashion, this must be one of the most creative concepts. You can also buy ready-cut lycra cotton clothes.

26. Antoine et Lili - Etnic Hippie Womenswear

51, rue des Francs Bourgeois   M° Hôtel-de-Ville
01 42 72 26 60   Mon-Sat 10.30-19.30
                      Sun 14-19.30
A W   €€

For details see Other Destinations.

27. Regina Rubens - Classic Womenswear

15, rue Pavée
01 44 54 07 04

M° St-Paul
Mon 13-19,
Tue-Sat 10-19, Sun 14-19

A W

€€

For details see the Montaigne - Fbg St Honoré

28. New York Industrie - Modern Men & Womenswear

19, rue Pavée
01 42 72 34 86
M W

M° St-Paul
Mon-Sat 11.00-19.30
€€

The new millennium brings change to Italian Diesel's line New York Industrie that was founded 1977. This new boutique is the first flagship store, and Kostas Murkudis, formerly Helmut Lang's assistant, has been brought in as artistic director. He leads a team of young designers that sets out to give the collection of basics a younger twist. The look is classic with a clean modern feel about it.

29. Paule Ka - Modern Chic Womenswear

20, rue Mahler
01 40 29 96 03
W

M° St-Paul
Mon-Sat 10.00-19.00
€€

For details see the Montaigne - Fbg St-Honoré.

29. Marithé et Francois Girbaud - Denim and Leisurewear

20, rue Mahler
01 44 54 92 44

M° St-Paul
Tue -Fri 10.00-19.00
Sat 11.00-19.00

W

€€

This recently opened shop sells the new demin concept from Girbaud. For details see Étienne Marcel - Les Halles.

30. L'Eclaireur - International Designer Wear

12, rue Mahler
01 44 54 22 11
A M

M° St Paul
Tue-Sat 11.00-19.00
€€€

This is the menswear shop. For details see no 37 this chapter.

31. Culotte - Trendy Womenswear

7, rue Mahler
01 42 71 58 89

W

M° St-Paul
Sun13-19,
Tue-Sat 11-19
€€

Japanse Yasuyuki Nakazono and Minako Ito are the design duo behind the label Poids Net that takes you back to the 1970 and 80s. Trashed t-shirts, flounced skirts and checked jackets come in vivid colours and period prints. The retro style, although, is more than just a nostalgic trip to the age of the legwarmers, thanks to a strong modern attitude. The printed panties are a hit.

32. Anna Kaszer - Contemporary Womenswear

7, rue Mahler
01 40 27 90 10
A W

M° St-Paul
Mon-Sat 11-19.30, Sun 14-19
€€

Anna Kaszer made accessories for Mugler, Lolita Lempicka and Kenzo before starting her own business. She does sweaters, tops, shirts and handbags with an ethnic flavour. Rich in colour, the clothes reflect her Celtic and Eastern European roots. Reasonably priced.
Also at: 16, rue de Turenne (this chapter).

33. Comptoir Des Cotonniers - Basics

18, rue Saint Antoine
01 40 27 09 08
W

M° Bastille
Mon-Sat 10.00-19.00
€

For details see St-Germain.

34. ICB - Urban Chic Womenswear

2, rue des Rosiers
01 49 96 61 00
W

M° St-Paul
Mon-Sat 10.30-19
€€€

Japanse ICB, short for International Concept Brand, has recently enlisted Dutch avant-garde duo Victor & Rolf to breathe new life into the label. The look is classic but playful, a mix of timeless pieces with modern forward-thinking styles. Signature features are bumblebee prints and buttons, and wave pockets. Definitely worth checking out for the fashion-savvy woman over 25.

35. Paoula Frani - Fashionable Womenswear

3 bis, rue des Rosiers
01 42 74 65 66
A W

M° St-Paul
Sun-Mon 15-19, Tue-Sat 11-19
€€€

Italian designer Paoula Frani creates clothes for the working woman who wants to look both elegant and sultry. The collections are built around trousers, especially with a masculine cut, and whatever the season, her favourite colour is black. The silhouette is skinny with hug-me-tight jeans; and a special feature of hers is underwear worn as outerwear. Shoes are modern and trendy.

36. Pleats Please - Issey Miyake's Second Line

3 bis, rue des Rosiers
01 40 29 99 66
W

M° St-Paul
Tue-Sat 10.30-19.30
€€

With Pleats Please Issey Miyake has once again taken innovation in fashion to a new level. Pleats Please's high-tech fabrics are first ironed into tight pleats, then fashioned into clothing and accessories. It's a traveller's wet dream that spells wrinkle-free, quick-dry clothes with a high comfort factor. The vibrant designs are inspired by traditional Moroccan clothing and come in plain colours, tie-dyed, tartan and even pseudo-denim. The pieces can be worn in a number of ways to create stunning shapes, lines and textures. *Also at: 201, bd St-Germain (St-Germain).*

37. L'Éclaireur - International Designerwear

3 ter, rue des Rosiers
01 48 87 10 22
A W

M° St-Paul
Mon-Sat 11.00-19.00
€€€

If international designer goodies are what you are after, this is a must. Armand Hadida's three boutiques are filled with all the established avant-garde labels be they Japanese, Belgian, Italian or French – Prada, Dirk Bikkemberg, Helmut Lang and Martin Margiela to name but a few. There is also a selection of interior design which includes plates by Fornasetti. The prices - no surprise if you're a heavy label junkie - are sky high. *Also at: 12, rue Mahler (menswear, this chapter), 26 avenue des Champs-Elysées (Montaigne-Fbg St-Honoré).*

38. Tiziana Pavan - Evening Wear

5 bis   Rue des Rosiers
01 42 77 91 22

W

M° St-Paul
Mon 13.30-19,
Tue-Fri 11-19
€€€

Tiziana primarily makes evening gowns and capes for weddings and other special occasions. The look is romantic with a gothic twist. The collection is made up of shiny or glittering fabrics such as satin, viscose or lurex. Add embroideries, spangles and gold trim and you're ready for the ball.

39. Martin Grant - Designer Womenswear

32, rue des Rosiers
01 42 71 39 49
W

M° St-Paul
Tue-Sat 13.00-19.30
€€€

Australian designer Martin Grant is a favourite among the hip fashion crowd for his cool Parisian chic style. His razor sharp cutting technique that gives the clothes such a clean strong silhouette, comes with fastidious but beautiful detailing. The elegant leather and suede jackets are a good choice. There is also a made-to-measure service, much in demand by brides-to be.

40. Jack Henry - Designer Menswear

54, rue des Rosiers
01 44 59 89 44
A M

M° St-Paul
Mon-Sat 14.30-19.30
€€

Inspired by street fashion and military basics, up-and-coming New York-born designer Jack Henry does urban menswear, such as asymmetrical overcoats, olive blousons and hunting jackets. The suits with elongated silhouettes and the mesh t-shirts continues the theme. In the collections you can also find some rock glam influences.

41. Bethsabée - Fashionable Accessories

12, rue F. Duval
01 44 59 39 10

A

M° St-Paul
Tue-Sat 11.45-19,
Sun 14-19
€€

Come here for the collection of artisan accessories – they are made of fine exotic materials such as horn and bone. If you are searching for that individual statement the good news is that only three or four pieces are made in every design.

42. Le Clan des Chineurs - Fashionable Denims

19, rue F. Duval
01 44 61 01 73

M W

M° St-Paul
Mon-Sat 12-20,
Sun 14-19.30
€€

When it comes to re-worked denim and other classic American basics Le Clan des Chineurs is a front-runner. With patches, colour lashing, spangles and lots and lots of rivets, designer Pascaline Audren's wild imagination transforms the jackets, t-shirts and trousers.

43. Serge Amoruso - Custom-made Handbags

39, rue du Roi de Sicile
01 48 04 97 97
A

M° St-Paul
Mon-Fri 10-19, Sat 14-19
€€€

Custom-made bags and accessories with that sought-after deluxe craftsmanship are what artisan leather-worker Serge Amoruso, formerly at luxury house Hermès, can supply you with. Exotic, original leathers and geometric forms in unexpected combinations are his trademarks, as is the pyramid-shaped bag made of pear tree, ostrich and titanium. For those who can't wait, there is also a ready-to-wear collection. Pop into the Roi de Sicile shop and see the master himself at work. *Also at: 81, rue des Saints Pères (St-Germain).*

44. La Copine à Teddy Bear - Romantic Womenswear

12, rue du Roi de Sicile
01 42 71 13 41
A W

M° St-Paul
Tue-Sat 14-19.00
€€

With both Parisian and Asian sources of inspiration, Yuikko Tamamoto mixes labels from different parts of the world. The look is young and romantic with an artisan feeling. There is also a selection of jewellery like butterfly necklaces, and handbags in girly but sophisticated styles, like the ones made of traditional Japanese fabrics.

45. Mamz élle Swing - Vintage Clothes

35 bis rue du Roi de Sicile
01 48 87 04 06
W

M° Hôtel-de-Ville
Mon-Sat 14.00-19.00
€€

A little shop packed with vintage clothes from all the top-designers, such as Christian Dior, Thierry Mugler, Guy Laroche, Hermès and YSL. The look is ultra-feminine with pretty dresses and skirts.

46. Azzedine Alaïa - Feminine Designer Wear

7, rue de Moussy
01 42 72 19 19
W

M° Hôtel-de-Ville
Mon-Sat 10.00-19.00
€€€

A true master of cut and volume, he has the skills to manipulate the female form, giving it the most flattering shape possible. It's not just the clothes that set Tunisian-born Azzedine Ala a apart; he take his own route in the world of fashion with private viewings only of his collections. You won't find an Ala a sign or any shop windows at his Marais mansion and you'll have to ring the bell to get into his Julian Schnabel-designed boutique. In the courtyard you find his sales shop.

47. Zadig et Voltaire - Urban Trendy Womenswear

12, rue St Cr. d. l. Bretonnerie
01 42 72 15 20

W

M° Hôtel-de-Ville
Mon 13-19.30,
Tue-Sat 10.30-19.30
€€

For details see Saint Honoré.

48. Accessoire Jean-Paul Barriol - Modern Footwear

36, rue Vieille du Temple
01 40 29 99 49
A W

M° Hôtel-de-Ville
Mon-Sat 11.00-19.00
€€

For details see St-Germain.

49. Selima Optique - Eyewear

46, rue Vieille du Temple
01 48 04 38 55

A

M° Hôtel-de-Ville
Mon-Sat 11-19.30,
Sun 11-19
€€€

At Selima Salaun's boutique you find luxurious eyewear in over 100 different styles. And if your lifestyle dictates that your glasses should never be seen on anyone else, she also designs frames especially for you - something she has done for celebs like Donatella Versace and Wiona Ryder.

50. FutureWare Lab - Avant-garde Dressing

64, rue Vieille du Temple   M° St-S-Froissart
01 42 23 66 08   Tue-Sat 11-19, Sun 16-19
M W   €€

Russian-born Tatiana Lebdev's clothes are for the 21st century woman who wants originality. She works with deconstructed designs and exposed seams in a tough-girl style, as seen in blazers with cut-away underarms, skirts that can convert into trouser jumpsuits or shirts with four sleeves. *Also see other destinations.*

51. José Lévy á Paris - French Designer Menswear

70, rue Vieille du Temple   M° Hôtel-de-Ville
01 48 04 39 16   Mon-Sat 12.00-20.00
M   €€

José Lévy creates suits, trousers and jackets with sharp masculine tailoring. The look which is softed by his sophisticated use of colour and detailing, is slightly coquettish and often the pieces bear sign of retro references. He is not afraid of borrowing a few elements from women's fashion. His non-derivative approach to fashion has won him much local praise and in Autumn 2002, he has opened in-store shops at Galeries Lafayette and Le Bon Marché.

52. Jean-Baptiste Rautureau – Trendy Men's Footwear

16, rue du Bourg Tibourg   M° Hôtel-de-Ville
01 42 77 01 55   Mon-Sat 11.00-19.00
M   €€€

For details see St-Germain.

53. Nim - Hip Jeanswear

16, rue du Bourg Tibourg   M° Hôtel-de-Ville
01 42 77 19 79   Tue-Sat 13-20, Sun 15-19
M W   €€

Nim (short for denim) is a gallery and jeans store in one. For denims pick up Levis Engineered, Red tab, Le Clan des Chineurs, or go for customized styles from Watanabe, Jeremy Scott and Gaspard Yurkievich. For matching footwear there's limited-edition Adidas trainers. Every month different young artists exhibit their work in the mini-gallery.

54. Anatomica - Comfortable Footwear

14, rue du Bourg Tibourg   M° Hôtel-de-Ville
01 42 74 10 20   Mon-Sat 11-19, Sun 14-19
M W   €€

Looking for shoes that put comfort first? This is where to go. Anatomica stocks the largest selection of Birkenstocks in Paris, as well as walking shoes from Alden and Walky, Blundstone and Trippen clogs.

55. Menkes - Drag- and Dance Clothes

12, rue Rambuteau   M° Rambuteau
01 40 27 91 81   Tue-Fri 10-17.30, Sat 10-19
M W   €€

Marais boutique Menkes, is famous for its glittering drag-queen outfits, but it also stocks a good selection of modern dance and flamenco gear, like leotards, tutus and tights. They also offer made-to-measure shoes.

56. Tsumori Chisato - Japanese Designer

20, rue Barbette   M° St-Paul
01 42 78 18 88   Mon-Sat 11.00-19.00
W   €€

This is the only shop in Europe that sells Tokyo-based Chisato's designs. The gallery-like interior, by hot architect Christian Biecher, is a spartan but tasteful contrast to the clothes that the former Issey Miyake assistant creates in a charming feminine mood. New materials are mixed with traditional ones in clothes with a soft silhouette.

57. Nicole Cadine - Feminine Womenswear

11, rue Elzevir	M° St-Paul
01 42 77 00 41	Mon 11-19, Sun 14-19
W	€€

In an old workshop with the original ironwork still intact, Belgian designer Nicole Cadine shows her romantic evening dresses and gala gowns. Taffeta and tulle in sophisticated violets, purples and black comes in supple, floaty silhouettes. Her pared downed everyday wear has a similar soft but more ethnic feel, with fur shawls, mohair jumpers, embroidered knitwear and a warm palette of colours.

58. Xuly-Bet - Funky Womenswear

16, rue Elzevir	M° St-Paul
01 44 54 55 88	Mon-Sat 11-14, 15-19
W	€€

Behind the fashion label, Xuly-Bet, is Lamine Kouyate from Mali. In the 1990s he was the king of street-savvy fashion with his African-roots mixed with Parisian-street-style influences, all made up of charity-shop findings, which he completely reinvented. A more sophisticated style has evolved, still with the trademark seams and label on the outside. Second-skin lycras and denims are favourite fabrics. *Also at: Forum des Halles (Étienne Marcel - Les Halles).*

59. C.Charon - Belgian Designer Menswear

4, rue de Perche	M° Filles du Calvaire
01 44 54 03 83	Tue-Sat 12-19
M	€€

Belgian menswear designer Christophe Charon doesn't let his roots affect him. No sign of the three-sleeved jacket or "any colour as long as it's black" Antwerp-designer musts. Charon prefers to play with vivid colours, simple figure-flattering cuts, and pays great attention to detail when he creates his relaxed urban menswear.

60. Karine Dupont - Modern Bags and Accessories

22, rue de Poitou	M° Filles du Calvaire
01 40 27 84 94	Tue-Sat 12-19
A	€€

Deep in the Marais district Karine Dupont makes bags that are clever and practical, yet modern with a distinctive look. Her bestseller is the three-in-one bag with detachable compartments – it comes in an array of colours and is made of satin, nylon or denim. She also works with leather, as in the pierced and frilled Woodstock line. Check out her accessories for pets, the perfect gift for any dog lover.

61. L'Habilleur - Discount Designer Shop

44, rue de Poitou	M° St Sébastien Froissart
01 48 87 77 12	Mon-Sat 11-20
M W	€€

This is said to be the hippest discount designer shop in Paris, favoured by those in the know. It may be so, but on many occasions the boutique seems full of endless racks of rather mediocre John Richmond items, and few pairs of shoes in size 45. In other words, to find the real bargains you need to have some luck to ensure that the fashion pack hasn't been there first. That said, it's still worth checking out. Last season's items are reduced by at least 50% for labels such as Jean Paul Gaultier, Ann Demeulemeester, Yohji Yamamoto, Patrick Cox amongst others.

6 & 7

St-Germain

With its classic cafés, Gauloises smoking intellectuals, jazz venues, small bookstores, and antique shops, Rive Gauche has all the attributes that make up the quintessential Parisian atmosphere you find here.

In the late 90s the St-Germain-des-Prés and adjoining areas in the 6th and 7th arrondissements, became the most sought-after areas in town. The big designer houses from the Rive Droite, Louis Vuitton, Dior, Emporio Armani landed, stirring mixed emotions in the area. But they haven't destroyed the atmosphere: what makes this area such a great fashion shopping experience is its diversity. The unifying theme is an artistic, intellectual approach to the good things in life. Be it fashion, books, bread, bed linen or flowers it's all about appreciating quality, not about instant label status. Yes, it doesn't always come cheap, but it's rarefied chic at it's best.

So, if you only have time to shop in one area – this is it. You find shops in every price range and for every taste, and if you share all fashionistas' obsession for accessories and shoes, this is as good as it gets this side of heaven! For that diversity you'll find small one-off boutiques such as Lebanese Liwan, and accessories designer Peggy Huynh Kinh as well as established designer names such as Sonia Rykiel, and Christian Dior. And Yves Saint Laurent was here long before it was the place to be.

For a well-edited mix of international designers, check out Onward, on boulevard St-Germain. For mid-priced fashion labels the choice is excellent, with Joseph, Paul and Joe and Vanessa Bruno amongst others.

The artery of the district is the Boulevard St-Germain, otherwise most of the streets are narrow. Too narrow for all the cars and lorries one can feel, walking the shoe streets rue Grenelle and rue Cherche-Midi. Besides that, the only downside is that the area has so much to offer. It takes some walking to explore it all. But if you take a break, relax and enjoy some people-watching at Café de Flore that fact won't hurt a bit.

Eating and drinking

Emporio Armani Caffé
149, boulevard St-Germain
01 45 48 62 15

Italian food with the same ambition as the designer clothes in the store that hosts this terrific restaurant. Best stop when doing serious shopping!

Café de Flore
172, boulevard St-Germain
01 45 48 55 26

The cliché of a Parisian café - here it is for real. A perfect place to watch the world and people, go by. No beret required.

L'Esplanade
52 rue Fabert
01 47 05 38 80

Brasserie de luxe. Fairly expensive, but good food and a nice view, facing the Esplanade in front of the Invalide dome. Very bourgeois clientele.

Bastide Odéon
7 rue Corneille
01 43 26 03 65

The bustling classic French bistro at its best.

Maxence
9 bis Bd du Montparnasse
01 45 67 24 88

A cosy Montparnasse restaurant with an ambitious menu and warm atmosphere.

Hélène Darroze
4 rue d'Assas
01 42 22 00 11

Paris' highest ranked female chef has brought the best of south-western French cooking to the capital.

Les Editeurs
4, carrefour de l'Odéon
01 43 26 67 76

During a long shopping day, take a break at this tranquil and cosy café. If hungry, there are some lighter dishes.

Staying

Hôtel L'Abbaye
10 rue Casette
01 45 48 07 86

If you would like a peaceful stay but still want to be right in the middle of both daytime and nighttime activities, Abbeye is a good choice.

Hôtel la Villa St-Germain
29 rue Jacob
01 43 26 60 00
www.villa-saintgermain.com

The French mother of the boutique-hotel trend. Established in the late 'eighties, but recently updated by Jean-Philippe Nuel, this hotel offers a discreet stylish stay. Mid-priced.

Hôtel Bel Ami
7 rue St-Benoit
01 49 27 09 33
www.hotel-bel-ami.com

One of the most talked about hotels, re-opened in 2000 in a very sleek, contemporary style It is rather large (115 rooms), but pay attention not all rooms have been redecorated

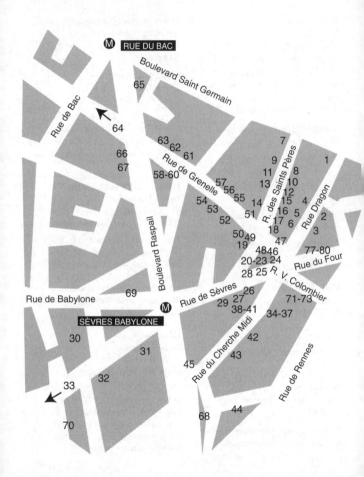

Rue du Dragon
1. Church's
2. Scooter
3. Demi-Lune
4. Lollipops
5. Stealth
6. Tod's

Rue des Saints Pères
7. Corrine Sarrut
8. Contact Plus
9. Paul & Joe
10. Capucine Puerari
11. Versus
12. Barbara Bui
13. Anne Fontaine
14. Salvatore Ferragamo
15. Y's
16. Hogan
17. Sabbia Rossa
18. Saints Pères Diffusion
19. Sportmax
20. Atsuro Tayama
21. Serge Amoruso
22. Anteprima
23. Paco Rabanne

Carr. de la Croix Rouge
24. Jean-Claude Monderer

Rue de Sèvres
25. Cécile et Jeanne
26. Falke
27. Losco
28. Furla
29. Dix-Sept
30. Le Bon Marché
31. Diapositive
32. Bally
33. Petit Bateau

Rue du Cherche-Midi
34. Camper
35. Givenchy
36. Robert Clergerie
37. Marithé & Francois Girbaud
38. Mare
39. Eres
40. Fausto Santini
41. Accessoire Jean-Paul Barriol
42. Agnès B Voyage
43. Lundi Bleu

Rue Coëtlogon
44. Peggy Huynh Kinh

Place Alphonse Deville
45. Joyce and Co

Rue de Grenelle
46. Yohji Yamamoto
47. Sonia Rykiel
48. Prada
49. YSL
50. Paraboot
51. MiuMiu
52. Martin Sitbon
53. Stephane Kélian
54. Patrick Cox
55. Sergio Rossi
56. Jean-Baptiste Rautureau
57. Iris
58. Emanuel Ungaro
59. Barbara Bui
60. Frederic Malle
61. Christian Louboutin
62. Cerrutti 1881
63. Michel Perry
64. Petit Bateau

Boulevard Raspail
65. Oliver Strelli
66. Kenzo

67. Paul Smith
68. Christian Lacroix (Bridal)

Rue de Babylone
69. Marithé & Francois Girbaud

Rue Saint Placide
70. Du Pareil au Même

Rue du Vieux Colombier
71. Claudie Pierlot
72. Marcel Lassance
73. Victoire
74. Agnès B
75. Formes
76. Zadig & Voltaire

Rue du Four
77. Marina Rinaldi
78. Et Vous
79. Diapositive
80. Paul & Joe Homme
81. Bill Tornade Enfant
82. Free Lance
83. MaxMara
84. Mosquitos
85. Tara Jarmon

Rue de Rennes
86. Zara
87. Céline
88. Kenzo
89. Burburry
90. Et Vous Homme
91. Mosquitos
92. H&M
93. Zara

Place du 18 Juin 1940
94. Mango

Rue Madame
95. Victoire
96. Irina Volkonskii

Rue Fleurus
97. APC
98. T. Yamai

Rue Bonaparte
99. Sequoia
100. Plein Sud
101. Joseph
102. BCBG
103. Cacharel
104. Apostrophe
105. Georges Rech
106. Lanvin
107. Stella Forest
108. Comptoir Des Cotonnier
109. Ventilo
110. Tiki Tirawa
111. Mandarina Duck
112. Mary Quant

Place St-Sulpice
113. YSL Rive Gauche Homme
114. YSL Rive Gauche Femme
115. Christian Lacroix
116. Séverine Perraudin

Rue Saint Sulpice
117. Agnès B.
118. Maria Mercié
119. Vanessa Bruno
120. Muji
121. Liwan

Rue Guisarde
122. Toni Truant

Rue Vaugirard
123. Antik Batik

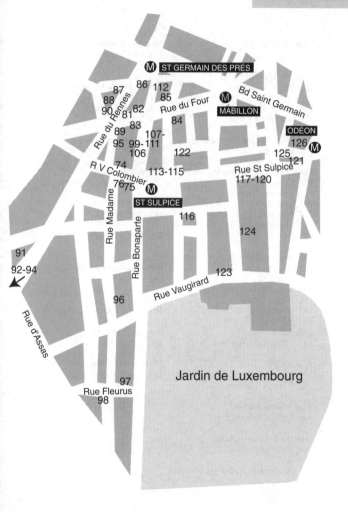

Rue de Tournon
124. Kathy Korvin

Rue des Quatre Vents
125. Pierre Talamon

Carrefour de l'Odéon
126. Christian Tortu

Boulevard Saint Germain
127. Diptyque
128. Be.You (K)
129. Du Pareil au Même
130. Onward
131. Emporio Armani
132. Lacoste
133. Sonia Rykiel Femme
134. Shu Uemura
135. Etro
136. La Perla
137. Regina Rubens
138. Apostrophe
139. Paule Ka
140. Sonia Rykiel Homme
141. Pleats Please
142. John Lobb
143. Bon Point
144. Baby Dior
145. Tartine et Chocolat

Rue du Bac
146. Missoni
147. Thierry Mugler

Rue Montalembert
148. Lucien Pellat-Finet

Rue du Près aux Clercs
149. Corinne Sarrut
150. Irié
151. Accessoire Jean-Paul Barriol

Rue de l'Université
152. Bon Point

Rue Jacob
153. Hervé L. Leroux
154. Corinne Cobson
155. Isabel Marant
156. By Terry

Rue de Seine
157. Geda. E-Pure
158. Antoine et Lili
159. Autour de Monde
160. Lagerfeld Gallery

Rue de l'Echaudé
161. Ragtime

Rue Saint Benoît
162. Upla

Rue l'Ancienne Comédie
163. Hugo Boss

Rue Buci
164. Comptoir des Cotonniers

Rue de l'Abbeye
165. Christian Dior

Place Saint Germain-des-Prés
166. Louis Vuitton

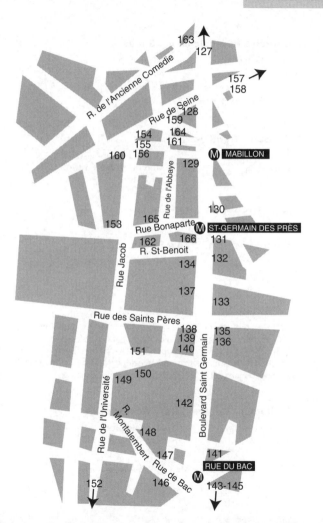

1. Church's - Classic Men's Shoes

4, rue du Dragon   M° St-Sulpice
01 45 44 50 47   Mon-Sat 10.00-19.30
M   €€€

For details see St-Honoré.

2. Scooter - Trend Jewellery

19, rue du Dragon   M° St-Germain-des-Prés
01 45 49 48 28   Mon 14-19, Tue-Fri 10-19,
                                          Sat 11-19
A   €

For details see Étienne Marcel – Les Halles.

3. Demi-Lune - Children's Shoes and Clothes

33, rue du Dragon   M° St-Germain-des-Prés
01 45 44 21 06   Mon 14-19.30
                                          Tue-Sat 10.30-19.30
C   €€

Two shops side by side, one with children's clothes, the other with
shoes to go with them. The shoes are the best buy and come in a
variety of styles and labels, such as Ralph Lauren Polo Sport, Chipie,
Coq Sportif, Moschino and Superega. The clothes have a sporty
casual look with jeans, t-shirts and sweaters. Besides their own label,
you can also pick up DKNY, Burberry and Polo Sport.

4. Lollipops - Contemporary Accessories

40, rue du Dragon   M° St-Sulpice
01 42 22 09 29   Mon-Sat 11.00-19.00
A   €€

For details see the Étienne Marcel – Les Halles.

5. Stealth - Clubwear

42, rue du Dragon	M° St-Germain-des-Prés
01 45 49 24 14	Mon 14-19.30,
	Tue-Sat 10.30-19.30
M W	€€

Come here for cool designer labels for both men and women. In the club music setting you can be sure to get in the right mood for young street smart designers such as Japanese Tsumori Chisato and crafty denim label Evisu. The label mix also brings you choice items from Fake London, Duffer, Aem Kei, Aem Aya and Earl Jean.

6. JP Tod's - Italian Leather Shoes and Accessories

44, rue du Dragon	M° St-Germain-des-Prés
01 53 63 39 00	Mon-Sat 10.30-19.00
A M W	€€€

This Italian label, maker of the popular pebble-sole driving moccasins, has become known for its casual-chic image, having graced the feet of celebs and royals since the mid 1980s. Although a cut below the top luxury brands like Hermès perhaps, Tod's shares their focus on classic yet modern shoes, bags and other leather accessories. Of course they always come with a hefty pricetag. *Also at 52, rue du Faubourg de Saint Honoré.*

7. Corrine Sarrut - Pretty Womenswear

42, rue des Saints-Pères	M° St-Germain-des-Prés
01 45 44 19 92	Mon-Sat 10.00-19.00
W	€€

You'll find wedding dresses here. For details see no 149 in this chapter.

8. Contact Plus - Streetwear

61, rue des Saints-Pères	M° Sèvres-Babylone
01 45 49 45 11	Mon-Sat 11.00-19.00
M W	€€

For sporty hip outfits Contact Plus has a cool mix of street wear labels. Pick up your gear from Lady Soul, Nike, K-Swiss amongst others.

9. Paul & Joe - Trendy Men and Womenswear

62, rue des Saints-Pères   M° St-Sulpice
01 42 22 47 01   Mon-Sat 11.00-19.30
W   €€

You'll find womenswear here. For further details see St-Honoré.

10. Capucine Puerari – Lingerie, Swimwear and Clothes

63, rue Saint Pères   M° Sèvres-Babylone
01 42 22 14 09   Mon-Sat 10.00-19.00
A W   €€

Capucine Puerari started out with lingerie in faded tones and floral prints in a very feminine, pretty style. This was a huge success and the collections expanded to womenswear, swimwear and accessories. The design is still romantic in style. The swimwear is well-cut in bold colours and retro prints. Today there is also a younger more affordable jeans line.

11. Versus - Versace's Diffusion Line

64-66, rue des Saints-Pères   M° Sèvres-Babylone
01 45 49 22 66   Mon 11-19,
                             Tue-Sat 10-19
A M W   €€€

Versus is limitless, no rules Donatella Versace's collections for serious young party-animals with a big wallet. In spite of the price tag, Versus can look a bit cheap and trashy; but the latest collections have shown a new freshness.

12. Barbara Bui - Trendy Womenswear

67, rue des Saints-Pères   M° St-Sulpice
01 45 44 37 21   Mon-Sat 10.00-19.00
W   €€

For further details see Montaigne - Fbg St-Honoré.

13. Anne Fontaine - White shirts for Women

68, rue des Saints-Pères   M° St-Sulpice
01 45 48 89 10   Mon-Sat 10.30-19.00
W   €€

This is a "one thing in a hundred different ways" shop. Anna Fontaine is all about white cotton shirts. The good quality shirts are made in France and come in classic, feminine styles – some trendier shapes can also be found. *Also at: 22, rue de Passy (Passy-Victor Hugo) and 12, rue des Francs Bourgeois (Le Marais).*

14. Salvatore Ferragamo - Italian Shoemaker

68, 70, rue des Saints-Pères   M° St-Sulpice
01 45 44 01 24   Mon-Sat 11.00-19.00
A W   €€€

For further details see Montaigne – Fbg St-Honoré.

15. Y's –Yamamoto's Diffusion Line

69, rue des Saints-Pères   M° Sèvres-Babylone
01 45 48 22 56   Mon-Sat 10.30-19.00
M W   €€

Japanese cult designer Yamamoto's second line for men and women is relatively unknown. In fact it has only been available in Europe for a few years, and is sold exclusively in the Yamamoto stores. It stands for a more wearable everyday Yohji style, with the same perfect technique but at half the price of the main line. *Also at: 25, rue du Louvre(Étienne Marcel - Les Halles).*

16. Hogan - Casual Shoes and Bags

71, rue des Saints-Pères   M° St-Germain-des-Prés
01 42 66 46 93   Mon-Sat 10.30-19.00
A M W   €€€

Hogan is the casual little sister of Italian JP Tod's. Though the label has been around since the 1980s, it is a recent revamping of the brand that has given it a considerable image boost. Hogan devotees swear by their casul-chic trainers for fantastic comfort. The footwear has rubber soles, and comes in soft leather or suede. Hogan also makes bags, the multi-coloured "Pan Am" vintage flight bag, has been snatched up by scores of celebs and American fashion editors.

17. Sabbia Rosa - Sexy French Lingerie

71-73, rue des Saints-Pères   M° Sèvres-Babylone
01 45 48 88 37   Mon-Sat 10.00-19.00
L   €€€

Sabbia Rosa is all about sexy French handmade silk lingerie. The big problem here is choosing from the wide variety of colours and prints - and paying the bill! Those who can - supermodels, actors and the like love it. Each panty or camisole is cut individually, hand-sewn with French seams, and always trimmed in silk lace. Garments can be made to order.

18. Saints Pères Diffusion - International Designer Wear

74, rue des Saints-Pères   M° Sèvres-Babylone
01 45 44 12 32   Mon-Sat 10.00-19.00
W   €€€

A small boutique that focuses on international designers such as Valentino, Moschino, Galliano and Vivienne Westwood. Francophiles are tempted with labels like Balmain.

19. Sportmax - MaxMara's Trendiest Line

72, rue des Saints-Pères   M° Sèvres-Babylone
01 45 49 22 03   Mon-Sat 10.30-19.00
W   €€€

MaxMara's younger sister Sportmax is the trendiest of the group's many labels. As with all the MaxMara labels, the team of designers is a closely-guarded secret. Here you can expect to find well-cut Italian tailoring with smarter fabrics and details, always in tune with the season's trends. Also worth checking out is the young casual line, Sportmax Code, with wardrobe basics such as jeans and t-shirts, 30 percent cheaper.

20. Atsuro Tayama - Japanese Designer

81, rue des Saints-Pères   M° Sèvres-Babylone
01 49 54 74 20   Mon-Sat 11.00-19.00
A M W   €€€

A Japanese designer, former assistant to Yamamoto and Cacharel, who sticks to the typical Japanese formula, though his clothes are always wearable and easy to grasp. His classy, elegant and comfortable creations come with new cuts and rounded shapes in sombre colours. Here you can also find the younger and less expensive Indivi line.

21. Serge Amoruso - Custom-made Handbags

81, rue des Saints-Pères   M° Sèvres-Babylone
01 45 48 29 41   Tue-Sat 11.00-19.00
A   €€€

For details see Le Marais.

22. Anteprima - Italian Designer Wear

81, rue des Saints-Pères   M° Sèvres-Babylone
01 45 44 44 41   Mon-Sat 11.00-19.00
A W   €€

The Milan based Japanese designer Izumi Ogino creates clothes with an Italian-Japanese expression, meaning simplicity and style in a discreet luxurious way. Clean colours and sharp tailoring are always at the forefront. Bags are slick, and in spring 2002 the label launched the first collection of watches, jewellery and sunglasses.

23. Paco Rabanne - French Designer Wear

83, rue des Saints Pères
01 45 48 82 97
W

M° Sèvres-Babylone
Mon 11-19, Tue 10-19
€€€

Paco Rabanne's design certainly is consistent. Since the sixties he has stuck to one thing - an ongoing desire for metals, whether it be hooks and eyes, zips or anything else shiny. It's a glittering space-age look, only for the brave babes, that seems to resist the laws of nature. One dress is entirely made up of white glass prisms. Black, white, red and needless to say, metallic shades are the preferred palette.

24. Jean-Claude Monderer - Contemporary Footwear

2, car. de la Croix-Rouge
01 45 48 78 54
M W

M° Sèvres-Babylone
Mon 10.30-19, Tue-Sat 10.30-19.30
€€

For details see Le Marais.

25. Cécile et Jeanne - Jewellery

4, rue de Sèvres
01 42 22 82 82
A

M° Sèvres-Babylone
Mon-Sat 11.00-20.00
€€

For details see St-Honoré.

26. Falke - Hosiery

5, rue de Sèvres   M° Sèvres-Babylone
01 42 84 22 08   Mon-Sat 10.30-19.00
M W   €€

German company Falke primarily does hosiery. Not as expensive as
Wolford, it's good for more basic pieces. They also have a selection of
modern relaxed ready-to-wear clothes and sportswear for both sexes.

27. Losco - Leather Accessories

5, rue de Sèvres   M° Sèvres-Babylone
01 42 22 77 47   Mon 14-19, Tue-Sat 11-13, 14-19
A   €€

For details see Le Marais.

28. Furla - Italian Leather Accessories and Shoes

8, rue de Sèvres   M° Sèvres-Babylone
01 40 49 06 44   Mon-Sat 10.00-19.00
A   €€

For further details see Montaigne – Fbg St-Honoré.

29. Dix-sept - Lifestyle/Fashion

17, rue de Sèvres   M° Sèvres-Babylone
01 42 86 98 28   Mon-Sat 11.00-20.00
M O W   €€€

The mega success of the cool mini department store concept à la
Colette has of course got its followers. But where Colette is about
high-status designer names, Carole Bona's Dix-sept is more about
displaying new young designer talents such as Yoss, Timotée Pic and
Arays Indra. A few more established designers also finds their way
here like Éric Bergère. Besides men and women's clothing, there is
also a selection of books, cosmetics and flowers.

30. Le Bon Marché - Department Store

22, rue de Sèvres
01 44 39 80 00

M° Sèvres-Babylone
Mon- Wed, Fri 09.30-19,
Thu 10-21, Sat 9.30-20

A B M O W

This Left Bank department store has always had an elegant and well-bred style reflecting its local customers. Now in the process of a face-lift things are hotting up considerably. Always refined and exquisite, it now stocks more cutting-edge labels such as Victor & Rolf, Martin Margiela, Ann Demeulemeester and Balenciaga. To boost the shopping experience further there is a slick perfumery and an enormous lingerie department. If you and your credit card can make it to the accessories there's Tod's, Louis Vuitton, Gucci and Ferragamo to complete your label gluttony.

31. Diapositive - Fashionable Womenswear

33, rue de Sèvres
01 42 22 00 45
W

M° Sèvres-Babylone
Mon 12.30-19, Tue-Sat 10.30-19
€

For details see St-Honoré.

32. Bally - Urban Chic Shoes and Bags

45, rue de Sèvres
01 44 39 17 15
A

M° Sèvres-Babylone
Mon-Sat 10.00-19.00
€€€

At rue de Sèvres you'll find bags, shoes for men and women. The flagship store is situated at 35, bd des Capucines. For details see Opéra.

33. Petit Bateau – Children's Clothes and Womens t-shirts

81, rue de Sèvres
01 45 49 48 38
C

M° Sèvres-Babylone
Mon-Sat 10.00-19.00
€

Basic and comfortable designs in soft colours are what you get with this label, which has been going on for more than 100 years. In the nineties the T-shirts where snapped up by hip young Parisians who loved the tiny soft-cotton V and round necks in colours such as lemon and pale blue. *Petit Bateau has 13 branches in Paris for example: 161, rue de Grenelle, 116, avenue des Champs-Elysées, 13, rue Tronchet, 64, avenue Victor Hugo.*

34. Camper - Casual Footwear

1, rue du Cherche-Midi   M° St-Sulpice
01 45 48 22 00   Mon-Sat 10.00-19.00
M W   €€

For details see Montaigne – Fbg St-Honoré.

35. Givenchy - French Couturier

5, rue du Cherche-Midi   M° Sèvres-Babylone
01 45 44 37 95   Mon-Sat 10.00-19.00
A M W   €€€

This shop sells accessories. For details see Montaigne – Fbg St Honoré.

36. Robert Clergerie -French Designer Shoes

5, rue du Cherche-Midi   M° St-Sulpice
01 45 48 75 47   Mon-Sat 10.00-19.00
M W   €€€

Robert Clergerie, the grand old man of French shoemaking, keeps turning out footwear that speaks to classic good taste as well as the more fashion-conscious spirits. His style of modern classicism has a grown-up feeling, but still with that little touch of sex appeal to keep it interesting. The shoes are always comfortable to wear - with or without the signature elongated toe. *Also at: 46, rue Croix des Petits Champs (Étienne Marcel - Les Halles), 18, avenue Victor Hugo (Passy-Victor Hugo).*

37. Marithé & Francois Girbaud - Denim and Leisurewear

7, rue du Cherche midi
01 53 63 53 63

M° Sèvres-Babylone
Tue-Fri 10.00-19.00
Sat 11.00-19.00

M W
€€

This huge left bank flagship store opened in 2002 and is worth a visit only for its decor. For details see Étienne Marcel – Les Halles.

38. Mare - Italian Fashion Shoes

4, rue du Cherche-Midi
01 45 44 55 33

M° St-Sulpice
Mon 14-19,
Tue-Sat 11-19.30

M W
€€

For details see Le Marais.

39. Eres - Sophisticated Swimwear and Lingerie

4 bis, rue du Cherche-Midi
01 45 44 95 54
W

M° Sèvres-Babylone
Mon-Sat 10.00-19.00
€€€

For details see Montaigne – Fbg St-Honoré.

40. Fausto Santini - Italian Designer Shoes

4 ter, rue du Cherche-Midi
01 45 44 39 40

M° St-Sulpice
Mon 11-19,
Tue-Sat 10-19

A M W
€€€

Italian shoe designer Fausto Santini makes sophisticated luxury shoes for footwear cognoscenti. He is not a trend- follower but keeps to his own, original style with clean lines and refined simplicity. The shoes are made of ultra-soft leather in natural colours and they don't just look good; since Santini also cares about comfort, they feel good too. The trademark loop down the back of each shoe, is often present on his exquisite handbags that are both original and modern. Japanese designer teams are devoted Santini fans.

41. Accessoire Jean-Paul Barriol - Modern Footwear

6, rue du Cherche-Midi   M° Sèvres-Babylone
01 45 48 36 08   Mon-Sat 11.00-19.00
A W   €€

Jean-Paul Barriol is all about mid-priced, modern footwear and accessories. The quality is high and all items are manufactured in France. There is a good range of belts and handbags. The boots and shoes are the best bet here. *Also at: 8, rue du Jour (Étienne Marcel - Les Halles), 36, rue du Vieille du Temple (Le Marais), 11, rue du Pré aux Clercs (this chapter).*

42. Agnès b. Voyage - French Casual Chic

15, rue du Cherche-Midi   M° Sèvres-Babylone
01 44 39 02 60   Mon-Sat 10.00-19.00
A   €€

This shop sells luggage and travel accessories. For details see Étienne Marcel – Les Halles.

43. Lundi Bleu - Fashionable Shoes

23-25, rue du Cherche-Midi   M° St-Sulpice
01 42 22 47 94   Mon-Sat 11.00-19.00
A W   €

This is the second line of Accessoire Jean-Paul Barriol. Same designer, same fashionable look, the difference is that the Lundi Bleu shoes are made in Spain and are 40 percent cheaper than the mainline. Choose from classical styles as well as more trendy ones.

44. Peggy Huynh Kinh - Chic Handbags

11, rue Coëtlogon   M° Sèvres-Babylone
01 45 63 48 17   Mon-Sat 10.00-19.00
A   €€

Former architect Peggy Huyn Kinh designs for Cartier and other big luxury labels. For her own line of handbags the style is sleek, pared-down chic with a timeless feel to it. She also does minimalist jewellery.

45. Joyce and Co - Modern Accessories

1, place Alphonse Deville
01 42 22 05 69

A

M° Sèvres-Babylone
Mon 14-19.30,
Tue-Sat 10.30-19.30

€€

Joyce Quinion's handbags comes in all sizes and styles for both mother and daughter. In keeping with it's location, the style leans toward classic bourgeois tastes with a fashionable twist. You also find labels such as Peggy Huynh Kinh and Jamin Puech, who turn up the fashion level. She also stocks less expensive labels like Antik Batik and purses, sunglasses and other accessories.

46. Yohji Yamamoto - Japanese Designer

3, rue de Grenelle
01 42 84 28 87
A M W

M° Sèvres-Babylone
Mon-Sat 10.30-19.00

€€€

Since his revolutionary collections at the beginning of the 1980s, Yamamoto has been at the fashion forefront with his elegant, time-less, both wild and austere clothes. He still takes inspiration from the male wardrobe, pairing it with sharp silhouettes, asymmetry and neutral colours. For a while now his collections have had a sporty theme, and in his very personal way he excels in the art of making basics elegant. Clothes such as zip track suit and parkas are typical for the look that he - as always - brings together with a truly masterful touch. The collaboration with Adidas has resulted in much-wanted cool boxing shoes and trainers.

47. Sonia Rykiel Enfant - Designer Children's Clothes

4, rue de Grenelle
01 49 54 61 10
C

M° St-Sulpice
Mon-Sat 10.30-19.30

€€€

For further details see boulevard St-Germain.

47. Sonia Rykiel Femme - French Designer Wear

6, rue de Grenelle   M° St-Sulpice
01 49 54 61 00   Mon-Sat 10.30-19.00
A W   €€€

You'll find womenswear here. See boulevard St Germain for details.

47. Sonia Rykiel Chaussures - French Designer Shoes

8, rue de Grenelle   M° St-Sulpice
01 49 54 61 15   Mon-Sat 10.30-19.00
W   €€€

See boulevard St-Germain for further details.

48. Prada - Italian Designer Wear and Accessories

3 ,5, 9, rue de Grenelle   M° Sèvres-Babylone
01 45 48 53 14   Mon 11-19,
                                     Tue-Sat 10-19
A W   €€€

In the three Grenelle boutiques you find womenswear, shoes, bags
and leather accessories. The largest Paris store is in the 8th arrondissement on 10, avenue Montaigne. At 6, rue Faubourg de Saint
Honoré there is new shop selling womenswear and accessories. For
further details, see Montaigne - Fbg St-Honoré.

49. Yves Saint Laurent - Designer Shoes and Accessories

9, rue de Grenelle   M° St-Sulpice
01 45 44 39 01   Mon 11-19,
                                     Tue-Sat 10.30-19
A M W   €€€

A full-range YSL shoes and accessories boutique with many of the
must-have-items that YSL has created under Tom Ford's direction.
Although there are some everyday style shoes, this is primarily footwear that spells cosmopolitan glamour chic. For further details see
no 114 this chapter.

50. Paraboot - Classic and Casual Footwear

9, rue de Grenelle   M° Sèvres-Babylone
01 45 49 24 26   Mon 14-19,
                          Tue-Sat 10-19
M W   €€

For three generations the Richard-Pontvert family has been success-fully making their durable, quality shoes and boots. Don't expect to find any fashionable killer-heels here. Paraboot is all about classic, casual and comfortable footwear. *Also at: 13, rue Vignon (Opéra).*

51. Miu Miu - Prada's Second Line

16, rue de Grenelle   M° Sèvres-Babylone
01 53 63 20 30   Mon-Sat 10.00-19.00
A M W   €€

Miu Miu is Prada's younger line so called after Miuccia Prada's childhood nickname. The label certainly feels like a younger sister - more bohemian, and freer in spirit. Witty details, innovative fabrics and peculiar prints and colour combinations are at work here crea-ting that much sought after Prada formula of androgynity, romanti-cism and urban cool. But what's not negotiable is that the Miu-Miu girl and boy have to have slim figures. The good part, though, is that it's 30 percent cheaper than the mainline so be sure to check out the accessories.

52. Martine Sitbon - French Designer Wear

13, rue de Grenelle   M° St-Sulpice
01 44 39 84 44   Mon-Sat 10.30-19.00
M W   €€€

A favourite among fashion pros, Martine Sitbon successfully masters the Parisian art of pulling a look together from many disparate ele-ments. She started out as the wild child in French fashion, and still her cool clothes combine that rock chic with historic references and feminine romanticism. In the slick orange and purple Grenelle bou-tique you also find menswear with that same edgy attitude.

53. Stephane Kélian - Fashionable Shoes

13 bis, rue de Grenelle   M° Sèvres-Babylone
01 42 22 93 03   Mon-Sat 10.00-19.00
M W   €€€

Highly fashionable footwear, with its own distinctive style very much
sums up Stephane Kélian. It was back in 1977 that he got hooked on
fashionable designs, and the family company launched the line for
women. Even before that the Kélian brothers delivered men's shoes
with the much-appreciated signature hand-woven leather. This is
the flagship store that also stocks the men's line and the collection
he designs for labels such as Martine Sitbon and Jean-Paul Gaultier.
*Also at: 26, avenue des Champs-Elysées, 5, rue du Faubourg Saint Honoré
(Montaigne – Fbg St-Honoré), 20 avenue Victor Hugo (Passy – Victor
Hugo).*

54. Patrick Cox - Designer Shoes

21, rue de Grenelle   M° Sèvres-Babylone
01 45 49 24 28   Mon-Sat 10.00-19.00
M W   €€€

For details see Étienne Marcel – Les Halles.

55.Sergio Rossi - Italian Footwear

22, rue de Grenelle   M° Sèvres-Babylone
01 42 84 07 24   Mon-Sat 10.30-19.00
A W   €€€

Sergio Rossi, owned by the Gucci group, has been making shoes for
more than 30 years and keeps fashion junkies coming for that fabulous
shoe fix. Keeping an eye closely on the trends of the moment, the shoes
still have that classic feminity to them. Pair that with a high comfort
level - as high it can be with high-heels, of course - and you can see
why the canvas boots with brown leather side straps and the lizard-skin
ankle-strapped shoes with bone trim are selling like hot cakes. Rossi has
a weakness for anything that shimmers and shines so you can always

find metallic shades, especially snakeskin, in the collections. *Also at. 11, rue du Faubourg Saint Honoré (Montaigne - Fbg St-Honoré)*

56. Jean-Baptiste Rautureau -Trendy Men's Footwear

24, rue de Grenelle   M° Sèvres-Babylone
01 45 49 95 83   Mon-Sat 11.00-19.00
A M   €€€

If you think that men's shoes are a predictable rather dull story, check out the Free Lance offspring, Rautureau. His men's line is for cool lads who want to make a loud fashion statement – patent leather lace-ups with pastel stripes; snakeskin or printed loafers – all high-quality and made in France. For the not so daring there are also less provocative styles, but still with that special edge to them. *Also at: 16, rue du Bourg-Tibourg (Le Marais).*

57. Iris - Designer Shoes

28, rue de Grenelle   M° Sèvres-Babylone
01 42 22 89 81   Mon-Sat 10.30-19.00
W   €€€

Don't let the rather gloomy interior fool you, this is a treasure-trove for serious shoe-addicts. Iris is the name of the Italian factory that makes shoes for Marc Jacobs, Ernesto Esposito, Allessandro dell'Acua and Veronique Branquino – the very labels you'll find in this shop. As you have already figured out – the shoes are absolutely stunning.

58. Emanuel Ungaro - French Couturier

33, rue de Grenelle   M° Rue du Bac
01 45 44 02 09   Mon-Sat 10.30-19.00
A W   €€€

You'll find accessories in this shop. For more details see Montaigne – Fbg St-Honoré.

59. Barbara Bui - Trendy Womenswear

35, rue de Grenelle   M° St-Sulpice
01 45 44 37 21   Mon-Sat 10.00-19.00
W   €€

For further details see St-Honoré.

60. Editions de Parfums Frederic Malle - Scent

37, rue de Grenelle   M° St-Sulpice
01 42 22 77 22   Mon-Sat 11.00-19.00
B   €€€

If you don't want to smell like your friends check out Frederic Malle's small fragrance boutique. In the ultra-modern setting, designed by Olivier Lempereur and Andrée Putman, he showcases nine bewitching perfumes created exclusively for this boutique by some of the world's most respected perfume-makers.

61. Christian Louboutin - Designer Shoes

38-40, rue de Grenelle   M° Sèvres-Babylone
01 42 22 33 07   Mon-Sat 10.30-19.00
W   €€€

For details see St-Honoré.

62. Cerrutti 1881 - Italian Designer Wear

42, rue de Grenelle   M° Rue du Bac
01 42 22 92 28   Mon-Sat 10.00-19.30
M W   €€€

Once best-known for menswear that spelled serious suiting, Cerrutti's fashion cred has risen under the direction of womenswear designer Peter Speliopoulos. His Arte line (for day and evening wear) is characterised by clean modern shapes, deluxe fabrics and great attention to detail. The men's line is still alive and kicking with up-to date office and weekend clothes. For summer 2003 new designer Istvan Francer goes for a slim, modern look inspired by the Cerrutti heri-

tage. Also at: 27, rue Royal (men); 48, rue Pierre Charron (men); 15, place de la Madeleine; 17 (women) (Montaigne - Les Halles); 17 av Victor Hugo (women) (Passy - Victor Hugo).

63. Michel Perry – Discount Designer Shoes

42, rue de Grenelle
01 42 84 12 45
A M W

M° Sèvres-Babylone
Mon-Sat 11.00-19.00
€€

Here you'll find Stephan, the diffusion line by Michel Perry, and you can buy this and the main line shoes at half the price. The shoes and boots are from the same season last year and is a must for price-conscious fashion victims. For more details see Étienne Marcel - Les Halles.

64. Petit Bateau – Children' Clothes and Womens T-shirts

161, rue de Grenelle
01 47 05 18 51

C W

M° La Tour-Maubourg
Mon 11-19,
Tue-Sat 10-19
€

For details see St-Germain.

65. Oliver Strelli - Italian Men and Womenswear

7, boulevard Raspail
01 45 44 77 17

M W

M° Rue du Bac
Mon 12-19,
Tue-Sat 11-19
€€

Italian Oliver Strelli, born in the Belgian Congo, makes comfortable, wearable clothes in a relaxed modern style. Inspired by the colours of Africa, the collections are made up of casual trousers, jackets and shirts. The women's lines have more fashionable shapes and cuts, but get a personal twist with the prints and juicy colours.

66. Kenzo - French Designer Wear

16-17, boulevard Raspail   M° Rue du Bac
01 42 22 09 38   Mon-Sat 10.00-19.00
A M O W   €€€

For more than 30 years Kenzo Takada made wearable, young-spirited collections with a brilliant mix of colours, textures and patterns. Since 1999 when he retired, the designers Gilles Rosier and Roy Krejberg have managed the women and men's lines respectively. Kenzo aficionados have every reason to be pleased with their modern interpretation of the Kenzo look in items that combine an exotic vibrant touch with a sophisticated urban utility wear feeling. Kenzo Jungle is the purse-friendly second line. There is also the Kenzo jeans line. *Also in Montaigne - St Honoré, Passy - Victor Hugo, Étienne Marcel - Les Halles.*

67. Paul Smith - British Designer Wear

22, boulevard Raspail   M° Rue du Bac
01 42 84 15 30   Mon-Sat 10.30-19.30
A M W   €€

In 1976 he showed his debut collection in Paris, and today, 25 years later, Paul Smith is a worldwide success with an annual turnover of more than €200 millions. His truly personal designs combine classic items such as a navy-blue suit with a quirky British sense of humour - a bright floral lining. As he himself puts it, "Paul Smith is best described as Saville Row meets Mr Bean". He pays great attention to detail and play with unconventional colours and patterns as seen in his trademark shirts. This is the only Paris boutique.

68. Christian Lacroix (bridal) - French Couturier

66, boulevard Raspail   M° Rennes
01 42 22 13 04   By appointment only
W   €€€

For details see Montaigne – Fbg St-Honoré

69. Marithé & Francois Girbaud - Denim and Leisurewear

8, rue de Babylone
01 45 48 78 86
M W

M° Sèvres-Babylone
Mon-Sat 10.00-19.00
€€

For details see Étienne Marcel – Les Halles.

70. Du Pareil au Même - Children's Clothes

14, rue St Placide
01 45 44 04 40
C

M° St-Placide
Mon-Sat 10.00-19.00
€€

For details see Étienne Marcel – Les Halles.

71. Claudie Pierlot - French Womenswear

23, rue du Vieux Colombier
01 45 48 11 96
W

M° St-Sulpice
Mon-Sat 10.30-19.00
€€

For details see Étienne Marcel – Les Halles.

72. Marcel Lassance - Casual Menswear

17, rue du Vieux Colombier
01 45 48 29 28
M

M° St-Sulpice
Mon-Sat 10.00-19.00
€€€

For a relaxed, wearable and somewhat artsy look, Marcel Lassance is your man. He favours unusual fabrics with a loose cut silhouette. You'll find the whole wardrobe here. *Also at: 21, rue Marbeuf (Montaigne – Fbg St-Honoré).*

73. Victoire - Chic Menswear

15, rue du Vieux Colombier
01 45 44 28 14
M

M° St-Sulpice
Mon-Sat 10.00-19.00
€€

For details see Étienne Marcel - Les Halles

74. Agnès b. - French Casual Chic

6,12, rue du Vieux Colombier   M° St-Sulpice
01 44 39 02 60   Mon-Sat 10.00-19.00
A M W   €€

At No. 12 there is a menswear shop. For details see St-Honoré.

75. Formes - Maternity Wear

5, rue du Vieux Colombier   M° St-Sulpice
01 45 49 09 80   Mon-Sat 10.30-19.00
W   €€

For details see Étienne Marcel – Les Halles.

76. Zadig & Voltaire - Urban Trendy Womenswear

1,3, rue du Vieux Colombier   M° St-Sulpice
01 43 29 18 29   Mon 13-19.30,
                                Tue-Sat 10.30-19.30
W   €€

For details see St-Honoré.

77. Marina Rinaldi - Generous-sized Fashion

56, rue du Four   M° St-Sulpice
01 45 48 61 57   Mon-Sat 10.00-19.00
W   €€

For fashionable clothes in bigger sizes, look no further! Marina Rinaldi, part of the MaxMara group, makes high-quality clothing in fine materials with figure-flattering silhouettes in sizes 42-54. *Also at: 7, av Victor Hugo (Passy - Victor Hugo).*

78. Et Vous - Trendy Womenswear

46, rue du Four   M° St-Sulpice
01 45 44 70 21   Mon-Sat 10.30-19.00
W   €€

For details see Étienne Marcel-Les Halles.

79. Diapositive - Fashionable Womenswear

42, rue du Four
01 45 45 85 57

W

For details see St-Honoré.

M° St-Sulpice
Mon 12.30-19,
Tue-Sat 10.30-19

€

80. Paul & Joe - Trendy Menswear

40, rue du Four
01 45 44 97 70
M

M° St-Sulpice
Mon-Sat 11.00-19.30
€€

Only menswear here. For further details see St-Honoré.

81. Bill Tornade - Children's Clothes

32, rue du Four
01 45 48 73 88
C

M° Mabillon
Mon-Sat 11.00-19.30
€€

For details see Étienne Marcel – Les Halles.

82. Free Lance - Fashionable Footwear

30, rue du Four
01 45 48 14 78

W

M° Mabillon
Mon-Fri 10-19,
Sat 10-19.30
€€€

The Rautureau's brothers shoes really rock. Their trendy Free Lance collections give you everything from sky-high stilettos to square-toed pumps. With their wild creative imagination they make shoes that are kitschy, delicate or just plain sexy. The high-quality shoes are still made in the factory in Vendée which their grandfather started over hundred years ago. The men's line is sold under the Jean-Baptiste Rautureau label, but is not available at this shop. (see no 56). *Also at: 22, rue Mondétour (Étienne Marcel – Les Halles).*

83. MaxMara - Italian Elegant Womenswear

37, rue du Four   M° St-Sulpice
01 43 29 91 10   Mon-Sat 10.30-19.00
W   €€

For details see Montaigne – Fbg St-Honoré.

84. Mosquitos - Funky Footwear

25, rue du Four   M° St-Sulpice
01 43 25 25 16   Mon-Sat 10.00-19.00
M W   €

For details see Étienne Marcel – Les Halles.

85. Tara Jarmon - Contemporary Womenswear

18, rue du Four   M° St-Sulpice
01 46 33 26 60   Mon-Sat 10.30-19.00
W   €€

Modern, feminine, uncomplicated with lively colours and soft fabrics, Canadian Tara Jarmon's well-priced creations are a big hit. *Also at: 73, av des Champs-Elysées (Montaigne-Fbg St-Honoré); 51, rue de Passy (Pasy - Victor Hugo).*

86. Zara - Spanish High-Street Fashion

45, rue de Rennes   M° Rennes
01 44 39 03 50   Mon-Sat 10.00-19.00
A C M W   €

For details see Étienne Marcel – Les Halles.

87. Céline - French-American Chic

58, rue de Rennes   M° St-Germain-des-Prés
01 45 48 58 55   Mon-Sat 10.00-19.00
A W   €€€

For details see Montaigne – Fbg St-Honoré.

88. Kenzo - French Designer Wear

60, rue de Rennes
01 45 44 27 88
A W

M° St-Germain-des-Prés
Mon-Sat 10.00-19.00
€€€

For details see Boulevard Raspail this chapter.

89. Burberry - British Fashion

55, rue de Rennes
01 45 48 52 71
A M W

M° Rennes
Mon-Sat 10.00-19.00
€€€

For details see Montaigne – Fbg St-Honoré.

90. Et Vous Homme - Fashionable Menswear

62, rue de Rennes
01 42 22 25 54
M

M° Rennes
Mon-Sat 10.30-19.00
€€

This a new store with menswear only. For details see Le Marais.

91. Mosquitos - Funky Footwear

99, rue de Rennes
01 45 48 58 40
M W

M° St-Germain-des-Prés
Mon-Sat 10.00-19.00
€

For details see Étienne Marcel – Les Halles.

92. H&M - High-Street Fashion

135, rue de Rennes
01 45 44 30 00
A B C M W

M° St-Placide
Mon-Sat 10.00-19.30
€

For details see Étienne Marcel – Les Halles.

93. Zara - Spanish High-Street Fashion

140, rue de Rennes   M° Montparnasse Bienvenue
01 42 84 44 60   Mon-Sat 10.00-19.30
A C M W   €

For details see Étienne Marcel – Les Halles.

94. Mango - High-Street Fashion

3, place du 18 Juin 1940   M° Montparnasse Bienvenue
01 45 48 04 96   Mon-Sat 10.00-20.00
A W   €

For details see St-Honoré.

95. Victoire - Chic Womenswear

1, rue Madame   M° St-Sulpice
01 45 44 28 14   Mon-Sat 10.00-19.00
W   €€

For details see Étienne Marcel – Les Halles.

96. Irina Volkonskii - Creative Jewellery

45, rue Madame   M° St-Sulpice
01 42 22 02 37   Mon-Sat 10.00-19.00
A   €€

With her glitzy one-of-a-kind pieces the former assistant to Jean-Charles Castelbajac, Irina Volkonskii, has made a name for herself among the Parisian fashion-pack. Russian Volkonskii creates original pieces that are both cool and funny, like the rhinestone-covered whistles or the handcuff bracelets. She also does a cigarette brooch complete with smoke coiling from it.

97. APC - Fashion Basics

3-4, rue de Fleurus
01 42 22 12 77
M W

M° St-Placide
Mon-Fri 10.30-19, Fri-Sat 11-19
€€

Atelier de Production et Création's designer Jean Touitou must be obsessed with cuts and fabrics. He reinterprets wardrobe staples such as sweaters, V-necks and impeccably cut jeans in selected fabrics, making them among the best fashion basics around. The look is effortlessly hip with a good deal of attitude. Around the corner, at 45, rue Madame, you can pick up items from last season's collection at a 50-70 % reduction. There you'll also find Eley Kishimoto and a special collection of APC re-designs by British Jessica Ogden.

98. T.Yamai - Japanese Designer

7, rue de Fleurus
01 42 84 14 89
A W

M° St-Placide
Mon-Sat 10-13, 14-19
€€

This is the only European boutique that exclusively sells Japanese designer Yamai's collections. His quest is to make strong basics with a personal take, that he updates every season. Unlike many of his fellow countrymen he's not into the intellectual design approach. The well-made clothes are easy to grasp, but without being ordinary. The Japanese heritage can still be seen in the clean cuts and the low-key feeling.

99. Sequoia - Trendy Accessories

72 bis, rue Bonaparte
01 44 07 27 94
A

M° St-Sulpice
Mon-Sat 10.00-19.00
€€

A good choice for the fashion-aware on a budget, Sequoia, offers well-priced trendy handbags. There is an extensive range of sizes and styles to fit the season's trends and colours. Simply styled boots and moccasins add to the selection. *Also at: 6, rue Francs Bourgeois (Le Marais).*

100. Plein Sud - Trendy Womenswear

70 bis, rue Bonaparte   M° St-Sulpice
01 43 54 43 06   Mon-Sat 11.00-19.00
W   €€

For details see Étienne Marcel – Les Halles.

101. Joseph - Fashionable Womenswear

68, rue Bonaparte   M° St-Sulpice
01 46 33 45 75   Mon-Sat 10.30-19.00
W   €€

For details see St-Honoré.

102. BCBG - Trendy Men and Womenswear

66, rue Bonaparte   M° St-Sulpice
01 43 12 55 20   Mon-Sat 10.00-19.30
A M W   €€

For details see Opéra.

103. Cacharel - Trendy Men and Womenswear

64, rue Bonaparte   M° St-Germain-des-Prés
01 40 46 00 45   Mon- Fri 10.30-19,
                              Sat 10.30-19.30
A M W   €€

With British designer duo Clements Riberio this French label is back
in the spotlight again. They play with the Cacharel tradition of
French romanticism but give it a modern edge with asymmetrical
cuts, multicoloured stripes and other bold prints. It's a fresh young
look with chiffon tops, ruffled dresses and toreador trousers. The
accessories are also worth checking out. *Also at: 5, place de Victoires
(Étienne Marcel – Les Halles), 34, rue Tronchet (Montaigne – Fbg St-
Honoré), stock; 114, rue d'Alesia (not listed).*

104. Apostrophe – Elegant French Fashion

54, rue Bonaparte   M° St Sulpice
01 43 29 08 38   Mon-Sat 10.30-19.30
W   €€

For information see Montaigne – Fbg St-Honoré

105. Georges Rech - French Chic

54, rue Bonaparte   M° St-Germain-des-Prés
01 43 26 84 11   Mon-Sat 10.00-19.00
M W   €€€

For details see Montaigne – Fbg St-Honoré.

106. Lanvin - French Designer Wear

52, rue Bonaparte   M° St-Sulpice
01 53 10 35 00   Mon-Sat 10.00-19.00
AW   €€€

For details see Montaigne – Fbg St-Honoré

107. Stella Forest - Trendy Womenswear

61, rue Bonaparte   M° St-Germain-des-Prés
01 43 25 20 44   Mon-Sat 11.00-19.00
W   €€

Stella Forest is a good place to find urban funky clothes at affordable prices. It's a tough-girl chic look with wild mixes of fabrics: fake fur and nylon, denim and lace.

108. Comptoir Des Cotonniers - Basics

59 ter, rue Bonaparte   M° St Sulpice
01 43 26 07 56   Mon-Sat 10.00-19.00
W   €

Women of all ages come here for well-priced wardrobe basics. It's a simple, relaxed look with stylish details that pop up here and there in the collections. *Also at 30 rue Buci this chapter and in: Étienne Marcel - Les Halles, Le Marais, Passy - Victor Hugo and Other destinations.*

109. Ventilo - French Classic Womenswear

59, rue Bonaparte
01 43 26 64 84
W

M° St-Sulpice
Mon-Sat 10.30-19.30
€€

For details see Étienne Marcel – Les Halles.

110. Tiki Tirawa - Sophisticated Knitwear

55, rue Bonaparte
01 43 25 80 28
W

M° Mabillon
Mon-Sat 10.15-19.00
€€

Tiki Tirawa is all about knitwear. It's a sophisticated look with clean simple shapes in an array of fabrics - cotton, silk, cashmere or linen. The palette is sombre with a lot of white, black and some neutral tones complemented by seasonal colours. It's this kind of quality clothing that graces your outfit, whatever the trends and catwalks dictates. *Also at: 10, rue Cambon (St-Honoré), 41, ave Montaigne (Montaigne – Fbg St-Honoré).*

111. Mandarina Duck - Modern Luggage and Clothes

51, rue Bonaparte
01 43 26 68 38
A

M° Mabillon
Mon-Sat 10.00-19.00
€€

For details see Montaigne – Fbg St-Honoré.

Mary Quant - Make-Up

49, rue Bonaparte
01 43 25 03 96

B

M° St-Germain-des-Prés
Mon, Thu, Sat 10-19,
Tue-Wed 10-18
€€

British designer Mary Quant became world famous for her era-defining mini-skirts in the 1960s. This store mainly stocks the make-up range where you can snatch up her superb nailpolish in an array of funky colours.

113. YSL Rive Gauche Homme - French Designer Menswear

12, place St Sulpice
01 43 26 84 40

M° St-Sulpice
Mon 11-19,
Tue-Sat 10.30-19

M

€€€

The YSL man likes to play in cool, elegant suits with razor sharp cuts and slim silhouettes. For details see the YSL womenswear entry below.

114. Yves Saint Laurent Rive Gauche - French Designer

6, place St Sulpice
01 43 29 43 00

M° St-Sulpice
Mon 11-19,
Tue -Sat 10.30-19

A W

€€€

This, perhaps the most sought-after of fashion brands, was bought by the Gucci Group in 1999. The man with the Midas touch, Tom Ford, was made creative director, with the goal of achieving the same kind of turn-around as he did at Gucci. Of course, the Saint Laurent design is some heritage to build on. So far Ford has proved himself successful indeed, giving YSL's classics his own up-to-date sexy interpretations - the safarijacket, the caftan and of course "le smoking". *Also at: 38, rue du Fabourg-Saint-Honoré (Montaigne - Fbg St-Honoré); 19, avenue Victor Hugo (Passy- Victor Hugo).*

115. Christian Lacroix - French Couturier

2-4, place St Sulpice
01 46 33 48 95
C W

M° St-Sulpice
Mon-Sat 10.00-19.00

€€€

For details see Montaigne – Fbg St-Honoré.

116. Séverine Perraudin - Stylish Womenswear

5, place St-Sulpice
01 43 54 10 63
W

M° St-Sulpice
Mon-Sat 11.00-19.00
€€

In this quiet and pleasant Place St-Sulpice boutique you'll find Séverine Perraudin's simple stylish collections. The kind of no fuss clothes that once in your wardrobe you just can't live without. Formerly at Michel Klein, MaxMara and Missioni, she started her own label in 1988. The clothes are made in soft fabrics: jersey, tweed, cashmere and crêpes, as seen in beautiful knitwear and nice skirts.

117. Agnès b. enfant - Children's Clothes

22, rue St Sulpice
01 40 51 70 69
C

M° St-Sulpice
Mon-Sat 10.00-19.00
€€

For details see Étienne Marcel – Les Halles.

118. Maria Mercié - Stylish Hats

23, rue St Sulpice
01 43 26 45 83
W

M° Odéon
Mon-Sat 11.00-19.00
€€

For details see Étienne Marcel – Les Halles.

119. Vanessa Bruno - Fashionable Womenswear

25, rue St Sulpice
01 43 54 41 04
W

M° Odéon
Mon-Sat 10.30-19.00
€€

French Vanessa Bruno is favoured by those seeking hip but wearable clothes at reasonable prices. Her slimming trousers are winners with their leg-elongating cut. Even though the high-quality pieces incorporate cool details in tune with the fashion of the season, her designs rest on a clean, rather minimalist design aesthetic.

120. Muji - Japanese Basics

27-30, rue Saint Sulpice   M° St-Sulpice
01 46 34 01 10   Mon-Sat 10.00-19.00
B M O W   €

Muji means basic in Japanese, which sums up what you'll get here. The clothes as well as household essentials and stationery are well-designed and fairly priced. What they do best are the wardrobe staples such as socks and t-shirts. *Also at: 47, rue Francs Bourgeois (Le Marais), 19, rue Auber (Opéra), 51, avenue des Ternes (Other destinations).*

121. Liwan - Clothes and Homeware

8, rue Saint Sulpice   M° Odéon
01 43 26 07 40   Mon 14-19,
    Tue-Sat 10.30-19
O W   €€

This Lebanese boutique sells floaty loungewear in a "Mediterranean meets Arabian" style. Perfect for cool poolside relaxing, designer Lina Audi creates silk and linen djellabas, trousers and jackets in opulent colours or soft neutrals. Simple sandals and embroidered slippers go with the look. Beautiful cushions, candles, hand-blown glassware and bath products makes this a perfect place for gift-buying.

122. Toni Truant - Designer Menswear

19, rue Guisarde   M° St-Sulpice
01 46 34 67 70   Mon 13.30-19.30,
    Tue-Sat 10.30-19.30
M   €€

In this small, cosy menswear boutique you'll find a good selection of British-spirited quality clothes. There is a good selection of Paul Smith, and you can also equip yourself with items by Brit tailor Richard James as well as Ozwald Boatang, famous for adding life to strict English tailoring.

123. Antik Batik - Bohemian Chic

38, rue de Vaugirard
01 48 87 95 95
W

M° St-Sulpice
Mon-Sat 10.00-19.00
€€

For details see the Le Marais.

124. Kathy Korvin - Minimalist Jewellery

13, rue de Tournon
01 56 24 06 66

A

M° Odéon
Mon-Fri 10-19,
Sat 11-19
€€

Franco-American jeweller Kathy Korvin works with a minimalist
aesthetic, creating delicate plaited, and lacy-looking styles. Ostenta-
tion is forbidden here - purity rules. She uses semi-precious stones
and Swarowski crystals. Prices start at €22.

125. Pierre Talamon - Modern Menswear

17, rue des Quatre Vents
01 43 26 34 85
M

M° Odéon
Mon-Sat 11-13.30, 14.30-19
€€

The French designer Pierre Talamon's clothes have a modern relaxed
look. He uses vivid colours with a graphic quality to them, and the
silhouette is body-conscious and masculine. His biggest sources of
inspiration is the world of film along with music and the street.

126. Christian Tortu - Florals and Interiors

6, carrefour Odéon
01 43 26 02 56
O

M° Odéon
Mon-Sat 10.00-19.00
€€

One of Paris' most celebrated florists, famous for his fresh combinations of flowers, bark, moss and foliage. Nowadays Tortu also app-
lies his skills to the world of the interior, which you can see around
the corner at 17, rue des Quatre Vents. Here you'll find vases made of

zinc, stone or glass, and other things connected with flowers. There's also glass and china in a stylish rural mode. It's a perfect place for gift-buying.

127. Diptyque - Scented Candles

32, boulevard St-Germain
01 43 26 45 27
O

M° St-Michel
Mon-Sat 10.00-19.00
€€€

In the scented-candle capital, this is the original, still considered by many to be the best. Well ahead of the current trend for room scents – since the early 1960s to be precise – Yves Coueslant has been making wonderful-smelling candles. There are around 50 different scents to choose from, and they burn for 60 hours.

128. Onward - International Designer Wear

147, boulevard St-Germain
01 55 42 77 55

A W

M° St-Germain-des-Prés
Tue-Fri 10.30-19.30
Mon, Sat 11-19.30
€€€

In this light-filled store on three levels (formerly named Kashiyama) you'll find an immaculate mix of cutting-edge clothes, shoes and accessories. The selection includes European, Japanese or American designers most in vogue at the moment. Established avant-garde designers such as Victor & Rolf and Martin Margiela share space with Tom Van Lingen and other up-and-coming talents.

129. Be.You (K) - Funky Club Wear

150, boulevard St-Germain
01 43 54 08 46
W

M° St-Germain-des-Prés
Mon-Sat 10.30-19.30
€€

For details see Other Destinations.

130. Emporio Armani Fashion/Lifestyle

149, boulevard St-Germain   M° St-Germain-des-Prés
01 53 63 33 50   Mon-Sat 10.00-19.00
A B M O W   €€

If you want to grasp some of the Italian masters golden touch for half
the price of the signature label, this is where to go. This lifestyle "concept" store not only sells clothes with Armani's sophisticated clean
lines and soft fabrics, but also stocks CD's, books about fashion, art
and photography and glossy magazines. You also find jeans, Armani
Junior, shoes, accessories and lingerie. The lively restaurant on the
second floor is a good lunch spot with tasty Italian dishes. *Also at: 25,
place Vendôme (St-Honoré)*.

131. Lacoste - French Sports and Leisurewear

161, boulevard St-Germain   M° St-Germain-des-Prés
01 53 63 25 00   Mon-Sat 10.00-19.00
M W   €€

For details see the Montaigne – Fbg St-Honoré.

132. Du Pareil au Même - Children's Clothes

168, boulevard St-Germain   M° Mabillon
01 46 33 87 85   Mon-Sat 10.00-19.00
C   €€

For details see the St-Honoré.

133. Sonia Rykiel Femme - French Designer

175, boulevard St-Germain   M° St-Germain-des-Prés
01 49 54 60 60   Mon-Sat 10.30-19.00
A W   €€€

The French queen of fashion Sonia Rykiel epitomises Rive Gauche
relaxed chic. Her trademarks are jersey and knitwear, asymmetry,
ruffles and, of course, the cult stripes that go in every possible direction. Recent years have seen a growing hipness with younger and

flirtier collections. There is also a jeans line, and some of the often oversized accessories have been a major hit. *Also at 70, rue du Faubourg Saint-Honoré (Montaigne – Fbg St-Honoré), 6, rue de Grenelle, Kids 4, rue de Grenelle, Shoes 8, rue de Grenelle (this chapter).*

134. Shu Uemura - Japanese Cosmetics

176, boulevard St-Germain
01 45 48 02 55

B

M° St-Germain-des-Prés
Mon 11-19,
Tue-Sat 10-19
€€

When this shop opened in 1986 it set a new standard for beauty boutiques with its low-key design. Colour plays the lead here with an incredible palette of shades that you can combine as you wish in customized preparations. Uemura's natural style of cosmetics comes complete with a suitably minimalist transparent packing design. Every sales assistant is a trained make-up artist ready to help you find the perfect blusher or foundation. There is also a wide range of the finest beauty tools.

135. Etro - Italian Designer Wear

177, boulevard St-Germain
01 45 48 18 17
A M W

M° St-Germain-des-Prés
Mon-Sat 10-13, 14-19
€€€

This Italian family-run company is famous for it's extraordinarily crafted, brightly coloured paisley (Etro's hallmark), foulard and brocade ties. With it's bohemian deluxe look the label's fashion cred has been on the rise. Beside the prints, delicate fabrics such as tweed, silk, cashmere and wool, play the leading part here. The paisley scarves and shawls are bestsellers. *Also at: 66, rue du Faubourg St-Honoré (Montaigne - Fbg St Honoré).*

136. La Perla - Italian Lingerie

179, boulevard St-Germain
01 45 44 45 76
L

M° St-Germain-des-Prés
Mon-Sat 10.30-19.00
€€€

Lingerie that has all the Italian sex appeal you could wish for. La Perla stands for quality, in fabrics as well as in design and detail. There are several different lines; La Perla has the classic lace style, Maliza more modern fashion-inspired stuff and Marvel is the most x-rated. There is also a wide range of truly glamorous swimwear. *Also at: 20 rue Faubourg St-Honoré (Montaigne – Fbg St-Honoré).*

137. Regina Rubens - Classic Womenswear

182, boulevard St-Germain   M° St-Germain-des-Prés
01 40 20 03 61   Mon-Sat 10.00-19.00
W   €€

For details see Montaigne – Fbg St-Honoré.

138. Apostrophe – Elegant French Fashion

190, boulevard St-Germain   M° Rue du Bac
01 45 44 36 26   Mon-Sat 10.00-19.00
W   €€

For details see Montaigne – Fbg St-Honoré.

139. Paule Ka - Modern Chic Womenswear

192, boulevard St-Germain   M° St-Germain-des-Prés
01 45 44 92 60   Mon-Sat 10.00-19.00
W   €€

For details see Montaigne – Fbg St-Honoré.

140. Sonia Rykiel Homme - French Designer Menswear

194, boulevard St-Germain   M° St-Germain-des-Prés
01 45 44 83 19   Mon-Sat 10.00-19.00
M   €€€

Rykiel seems to be a wardrobe staple for Parisian men who work in creative professions – her leather clothes are especially attractive. Rykiel also does more classic sportswear and formal clothes, like suits and blazers.

141. Pleats Please - Issey Miyakes Second Line

201, boulevard St-Germain M° Rue du Bac
01 45 48 10 44   Mon-Sat 10.30-19.30
W   €€

For details see Le Marais.

142. John Lobb - Classic Men's Footwear

226, boulevard St-Germain M° Rue du Bac
01 45 44 95 77   Mon-Sat 10.30-19.00
M   €€€

Founded in 1849, Lobb is one of England's oldest and most famous makers of bench-made shoes, worn by the rich and famous. When Hermès bought the company in 1976 (except for the original John Lobb shoe shop on London's St. James's Street) they added high-quality ready-to-wear footwear collections. Only the finest leathers are used. The shoes are made in an artisan way, for example, the traditional British stitching on the bottom of the sole is done entirely by hand. *The store at 23, rue Boissy d'Anglas does made-to-measure. Also at: 51, rue Francois 1er (Montaigne – Fbg St-Honoré).*

143. Bon Point - Children's Clothes

229, boulevard St-Germain M° Solférino
01 40 62 76 20   Mon-Sat 10.00-19.00
C   €€

For details see Étienne Marcel – Les Halles.

144. Baby Dior - Designer Baby Clothes

252, boulevard St-Germain
01 42 22 90 90
C

M° Solférino
Mon-Sat 10.00-19.00
€€€

Baby Dior has a lot of irresistible clothes for little ones. It's not designed by John Galliano so you wont find any tribal warrior outfits here! Instead, what you get is safe but pretty items in nice colours and beautiful fabrics. It doesn't come cheap, but the Dior label is visible on almost every item, making it a perfect gift when the parents are the label-junkie type.

145. Tartine et Chocolat - Children's Clothes

266, boulevard St-Germain
01 45 56 10 45
C

M° Assemblée Nationale
Mon-Sat 10.00-19.00
€€

For details see the Étienne Marcel – Les Halles.

146. Missoni - Italian Luxury Knitwear

42, rue du Bac
01 45 48 38 02
A M W

M° Rue du Bac
Mon-Sat 10.00-19.00
€€€

For details see the St-Honoré.

147. Thierry Mugler - French Designer Wear

45, rue du Bac
01 45 44 44 44
M W

M° Rue du Bac
Mon-Sat 10.00-19.00
€€€

Since 1973 Thierry Mugler, has been creating his extravagant super-curvaceous clothes. His style ranges from vulgar ornamentalism to the most rigorous minimalism. He aims to reshape the body in a sexy, sometimes ironic, way. The clothes – be it a silk dress or a man's suit - are characterized by exaggerated shoulders, hand-span waists and a moulded silhouette. This is the flagship store that also stocks the less expensive Trade Mark line. *Also at: 8, place des Victoires (Étienne Marcel – Les Halles), 49, avenue Montaigne, 10, rue Boissy d'Anglas (Montaigne – Fbg St-Honoré).*

148. Lucien Pellat-Finet - French Luxury Cashmere

1, rue Montalembert   M° Rue du Bac
01 42 22 22 77   Mon-Fri 10-19, Sat 11-19
C M O W   €€€

The king of cashmere, Lucien Pellat-Finet has put fashion and rock'n'roll into this luxury fabric. A high-voltage clientele of models, fashion editors and celebs come for some of the finest cashmere in the world. Jumpers, chunky sweaters and twin-sets comes with quirky patterns such as camouflage, skull and crossbones, and the trademark pop and techno colours. Besides the flashy pieces there are also more conventional ones. There is also cute cashmere for kids and some homeware in the boutique designed by hot young Paris architect Christian Biecher, which is as playful as the collections.

149. Corinne Sarrut - Pretty Womenswear

4, rue du Pré aux Clercs   M° St-Germain-des-Prés
01 42 61 71 60   Mon-Sat 10.00-19.00
W   €€

Corrine Sarrut makes clothes that are best described as youthful and pretty with a 1940s mood to them. Lace, ruffles, pale colours and pearl buttons are typical of Sarrut items, like the floral print dresses and knit cardigans. Add her berets, and you have the classic French gamine look. *Also at: 42, rue Saints Pères (this chapter); 7, rue Gustave Courbet (Passy - Victor Hugo).*

150. Irié – Classic-Chic Womenswear

8,10, rue du Pré-aux Clercs M° Rue du Bac
01 42 61 18 28   Mon-Sat 10.15-19.00
W   €€€

Japanese Irié attracts the elegant Parisian avant-garde legions. Irié worked for Kenzo before launching his own label in 1983. The look is classic-chic, trademark features are the animal prints and the use of innovative fabrics and manufacturing methods. He uses laser cutting-techniques, a polyester and elastane mix that feels like a super-supple suede, and he has created a polyester crêpe suit that you can throw in the washing machine.

151. Accessoire Jean-Paul Barriol - Modern Footwear

11, rue du Pré aux Clercs   M° St-Germain-des-Prés
01 45 48 36 08   Mon-Sat 11.00-19.00
A W   €€

For details see no 41 this chapter.

152. Bon Point - Children's Clothes

65, 67, 86, rue de l'Université   M° Solférino
01 47 05 09 09   Mon-Sat 10.00-19.00
C   €€

At no 65 you'll find children's shoes. At no 67 women's clothes and at No 86 women and children's clothes. For details see Étienne Marcel-Les Halles.

153. Hervé L. Leroux - Sexy French Designer Wear

32, rue Jacob   M° St-Germain-des-Prés
01 55 42 00 39   Mon-Sat 10.00-19.00
W   €€

When fashion company BCBG acquired Hervé Léger's label known for sexy-bandage-dressing, Hervé himself was thrown out. He then changed his name to Hervé L.Leroux. And today his designs are still about tight-fitting sexy dresses in dramatic black or white.

154. Corinne Cobson - Parisian Club Fashion

1, rue Jacob   M° St-Germain-des-Prés
01 46 33 21 73   Mon 14.30-19.30,
                               Tue-Sat 10.30-19.30
B W   €€

For details see St-Honoré.

155. Isabel Marant - Bohemian-Chic Womenswear

1, rue Jacob   M° St-Germain-des-Prés
01 43 26 04 12   Mon-Sat 10.30-19.30
A W   €€

For details see Other Destinations.

156. By Terry - Personalized Cosmetics

1, rue Jacob   M° St-Germain-des-Prés
01 46 34 00 36   Mon-Sat 10.30-19.00
B   €€€

For details see Étienne Marcel-Les Halles.

157. Geda. E-pure - Streetwear

101, rue de Seine   M° Odéon
01 43 26 18 09   Mon 14– 19.30,
                               Tue-Sat 10.45-19
M W   €€

For details see Other Destinations.

158. Antoine et Lili - Etnic Hippie Womenswear

87, rue de Seine
01 56 24 35 81
A W

M° Odéon
Mon-Sat 10.00-19.00
€€

For details see Other Destinations.

159. Autour du Monde - Casualwear

54, rue de Seine
01 43 54 64 47

A M W

M° Odéon
Mon 11-19.30, Tue-Sat 10.30-19.30
Sun 13-19
€€

Serge Bensimon's Autour du Monde is the place where Parisians come for their holiday outfits. The clothes for both sexes have nothing to do with fashion, the collections consist of basics in natural fabrics. Inspired by travel and army clothes, the look is comfortable and relaxed with sporty colours, clean cuts and discreet detailing. Affordable prices. *Also at: 8, rue des Francs Bourgeois where you'll also find lifestyle and interiors in a pared-down style (Le Marais).*

160. Lagerfeld Gallery - Designer Fashion and Gallery

40, rue de Seine
01 55 42 75 50
A M O W

M° Mabillion
Tue-Sat 10.00-19.00
€€€

As the name implies this is both gallery and fashion boutique. The beautiful laid-back interior designed by Andrée Putman displays photographs, fashion and art magazines. Accessories by Lagerfeld and Fendi are here as well. In the basement accessed by a magnificent slate staircase, you'll find King Karl's signature lines for both men and women in a pared-down cool style. Look out for the deluxe denims made in cooperation with Diesel.

161. Ragtime - Vintage Couture and Ready-to-wear

23, rue de l'Echaudé   M° Mabillon
01 56 24 00 36   Mon-Sat 14.30-19.30
A W   €€€

This is one of the best vintage shops in Paris. Francoise Auguet sells both couture and prêt-à-porter from the 1880s to the 1970s, although she tends to specialize in the 20s through to the 50s. There is also a great selection of wedding dresses. Of course these things don't come cheap, but lower-priced accessories, hats, shawls and so on, can bring some comfort.

162. Upla – Lifestyle/Fashion

5, rue St-Benoit   M° St-Germain des Prés
01 40 15 10 75   Mon-Sat 10.30-19.30
A B M O W   €€

For details see Étienne Marcel – Les Halles.

163. Hugo Boss - Modern Menswear

19, rue l'Ancienne Comédie   M° Odéon
01 43 25 94 05   Mon-Sat 10.00-19.30
M   €€

For details see Montaigne – Fbg St-Honoré.

164. Comptoir des Cotonniers - Basics

30, rue Buci   M° St-Germain-des-Prés
01 43 54 56 73   Mon-Sat 10.00-19.00
W   €

For details see no 108 this chapter.

165. Christian Dior - French Couturier

16, rue de l'Abbaye
01 56 24 90 53
A W

M° St-Germain-des-Prés
Mon-Sat 10.00-19.00
€€€

For details see Montaigne – Fbg St-Honoré.

166. Louis Vuitton - French Luxury Leather and Clothes

6, pl. Saint Germain-des-Prés
01 45 49 62 32
A

M° St-Germain-des-Prés
Mon-Sat 10.00-19.00
€€€

For details see Montaigne – Fbg St-Honoré.

8

Montaigne - Fbg St-Honoré

When it comes to the 8th arrondissement, two things count: big designer brands and fat dollar wallets.

The super-elegant Montaigne area is home to all the classic French couture houses. With their unparalleled craftsmen's skills, elitism and bon gôut they are something unique in the more and more global world of fashion. But today the couture business serves mainly as a license and image-booster; the thing that keeps the rich and beautiful coming back for more is the deluxe prêt-a-porter.

Once this was the place to watch the "ladies who lunch" and you can still find women who don't shop anywhere else. But as stodgy labels have become hot again with new young designers, and international designers brands have moved in, this area has become more and more hip, or branché as the French would say. Today the area around the Champs-Elysées boasts some of the trendiest venues: chic restaurants, cool nightclubs and bars.

The main streets are avenue Montaigne, rue Faubourg Saint-Honoré, avenue George V and the adjoining rue Francois 1er. There you'll find almost all the big global designers in every style there is, be it Hermès or Roberto Cavalli. If your credit card is charged to the hilt, you can do as many others do in search of big designer drama: go for the diffusion lines, mostly aimed at a younger clientele and around half the price of the main line. Although it varies from label to label most of these lines are simply inspired by individual designers, not actually created by them.

A word of advice: some of the boutiques here are "très snob" and the sales assistants can be snooty - if you don't look like a million dollars. But don't be shy, just march right in with your head held high, brinning with self assurance, it usually does the trick. Wearing some visible status labels of course doesn't do any harm either.

Eating and drinking

Nirvana
3, avenue Matignon
01 53 89 18 91

Claude Challe's new restobar cum club is the most talked about glam-lounge in town. A perfect place to show your new paparazzi-attracting dress.

Market
15, avenue Matignon
01 56 43 40 90

Great contemporary cooking in a sober cool setting designed by famous Christian Liagre. A modern take on the classic upscale brasserie.

Korova
33 rue Marbeuf
01 53 89 93 93

Inspired by the bar in "A Clockwork Orange" this twisted restaurant is a great spot to have a drink after dinner.

Il Sardo
11, rue Treilhard
01 45 61 09 46

When it comes to Italian food, this is where you get best value for money in Paris.

Handmade

19, rue Jean-Mermoz
01 45 62 50 05

This chic venue offers home-made sandwiches, fresh salads and fruit juice in help-yourself packs.

Nobu

15, rue Marbeuf
01 56 89 53 53

The "stylish Japanese" concept has landed in Paris, looking better than ever.

La Cantine du Fbg-St-Honoré

105, rue du Fbg St-Honoré
01 42 56 22 22

Perfect for celebrating the picks of the day. From 18.30 to 20.30 a free buffet is served in the oh-so beautiful bar. Typical cross-over menu, minimalistic décor and trendy clientele.

Staying

Pershing Hall

49 rue Pierre Charron
01 58 36 58 00
www.pershinghall.com

Pershing Hall is an important newcomer to the more luxurious Parisian hotel scene. Beautifully designed by Andrée Putman, it also has a cool lounge bar and it is the perfect base for a luxurious weekend in the capital of style. Rates start at €380.

Plaza Athénée

25 Avenue Montaigne
1 53 67 65 00

One of the heaviest cornerstones in Mr Ducasse's global gourmet-empire. During the fashion weeks the hotel is the place to stay. Doubles start at €587, go for the top floor rooms that are decorated in a sober Art Deco-style.

Monna Lisa

97, Rue de La Boétie
01 56 43 38 38

Conveniently situated off the Champs Elysées, this converted 19th-century townhouse retains its elegant façade, combining it with a calm, sleek interior. Here you also find a stylish Italian bar and restaurant. Rates start at €191.

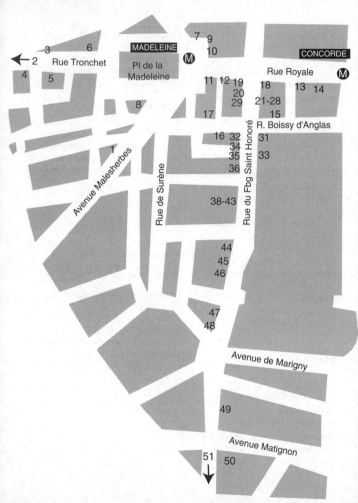

MADELEINE

CONCORDE

Rue Tronchet

Pl de la
Madeleine

Rue Royale

R. Boissy d'Anglas

Rue du Fbg Saint Honoré

Avenue Malesherbes

Rue de Surène

Avenue de Marigny

Avenue Matigny

Boulevard Malesherbes
1. Burberry

Rue Tronchet
2. Cacharel
3. Helion
4. Etam
5. Petit Bateau
6. Eres

Place de la Madeleine
7. Kenzo Homme
8. Cerruti 1881
9. Polo Ralph Lauren

Rue Royale
10. Adolfo Dominguez
11. Cerruti 1881
12. Chanel (shoes)
13. Bon Point
14. Daniel Swarowski

Rue Boissy d'Anglas
15. Thierry Mugler
16. John Lobb
17. Tartine et Chocolat

Rue du Faubourg Saint Honoré
18. Missoni
19. Gucci
20. Prada
21. Stephane Kélian
22. Jaeger
23. Sergio Rossi
24. Iceberg
25. Lolita Lempicka
26. Camper
27. Bottega Veneta
28. Lanvin (Menswear)
29. La Perla
30. Lanvin
31. Gianfranco Ferré

32. Hèrmes
33. Valentino
34. Givenchy
35. Yves Saint Laurent
36. Jitrois
37. Apostrophe
38. Christian Dior
39. Leonard
40. Salvatore Ferragamo
41. JP Tod's
42. Comme des Garçons
43. Chloé
44. Versace
45. Etro
46. Roberto Cavalli
47. Sonia Rykiel
48. John Galliano
49. Christian Lacroix
50. Walter Steiger
51. Tartine et Chocolat

Rnd. Pt. des Champs Elysées
52. Hugo Boss

Avenue des Champs-Elysées
53. L'Éclaireur
54. Stephane Kelian
55. Zara
56. Guerlain
57. Sephora
58. Tara Jarmon
59. Furla
60. Etam
61. Lacoste
62. Louis Vuitton
63. Petit Bateau
64. Bally

Avenue George V
65. Hèrmes
66. Armani Collezioni
67. Morabito

68. Gianfranco Ferré
69. JEY Store
70. Kenzo
71. Balenciaga
72. Givenchy

Rue Pierre Charron
73. Cerruti 1881

Avenue Pierre-1er-de-Serbie
74. Agnès B.
75. Leonard

Rue Marbeuf
76. Marcel Lassance
77. Berluti
78. Lanvin

Rue François 1er
79. Givenchy (menswear)
80. Morabito
81. John Lobb
82. Ermenegildo Zegna
83. Paule Ka
84. Frencesco Smalto
85. Versace
86. Courrèges
87. Balmain
88. Fendi
89. Thomas Pink

Rue Clement Marot
90. Scarlett

Rue de Marignan
91. Camerlo

Rue du Boccador
92. Apostrophe

Avenue Montaigne
93. Plein Sud
94. Emanuel Ungaro
95. Prada
96. Malo
97. Bon Point
98. Inès de la Fressange
99. Joseph
100. Regina Rubens
101. Montaigne 18
102. Dolce & Gabbana
103. Christian Lacroix
104. Christian Dior
105. Valentino
106. MaxMara
107. Tiki Tirawa
108. Emilio Pucci
109. Céline
110. Eres
111. Chanel
112. Salvatore Ferragamo
113. Thierry Mugler
114. 51 Montaigne
115. Calvin Klein
116. Marni
117. Loewe
118. Krizia
119. Barbara Bui
120. Jil Sander
121. Louis Vuitton

Avenue Franklin D. Roosevelt
122. Marithé François Girbaud

1. Burberry - British Fashion

8, boulevard Malesherbes   M° Madeleine
01 40 07 77 77   Mon-Sat 10.00-19.00
A C M W O   €€€

In the hands of president Rose-Marie Bravo the dowdy raincoat maker
has placed itself in every fashion-addict's wardrobe, with its edgy re-
interpretations of the classic check. After "Burberry fever" new designer Christopher Bailey, formerly at Gucci and Donna Karan, faces the
challenge of taking the label to the next level. His first official collection
for the Burberry's premium label, Prorsum, shows a younger approach
with a clever mix of sex appeal and modernity. And the over-exposed
check seems to have been abandoned - for now at least. This is the big
flagship store. *Also at: 55, rue de Rennes (St-Germain)*

2. Cacharel - Trend Womenswear

34, rue Tronchet   M° Madeleine
01 47 42 12 61   Mon-Fri 10.30-19, Sat 10.30-19.30
W   €€

For details see St Germain.

3. Helion - Gloves

22, rue Tronchet   M° Madeleine
01 47 42 26 79   Mon 13.30-19.45, Tue-Sat 10-19.45
A   €€

The fashion cognoscenti knows that it's the small details that make the
difference. The perfect pair of gloves, for instance. If that's your problem,
here's where you get the fix.

4. Etam - High-Street Womenswear

21, rue Tronchet   M° Havre Caumartin
01 40 06 05 93   Mon-Sat 10.00-19.00
C L W   €

For details see Étienne Marcel – Les Halles.

5. Petit Bateau – Children's wear and Women's t-shirts

13, rue Tronchet
01 42 65 26 26
C W

M° Madeleine
Mon-Sat 10.00-19.00
€

For details see St-Germain.

6. Eres - Sophisticated Swimwear and Lingerie

2, rue Tronchet
01 47 42 28 82
L W

M° Madeleine
Mon-Sat 10.00-19.00
€€€

Since 1968 women have loved Eres for its sophisticated low-key elegant swimwear and lingerie. If you want frills, flashy prints and colours - don't bother. What you get here are figure-flattering shapes in a large selection of styles and sizes. Tops and bottoms are sold separately. The swimwear look is French Riviera-chic with clean lines and muted colours in quality fabrics. The cruise collection arrives in November, and the summer collection in January. Lingerie is light with few but flawless details. *Also at: 40, avenue Montaigne, 4, rue du Cherche-Midi (St-Germain), 6, rue Guichard (16th, not listed)*

7. Kenzo Homme - French Designer Wear

10, place de la Madeleine
01 42 61 04 51
M

M° Madeleine
Mon-Sat 10.00-19.00
€€€

This shop sells menswear. For details see St-Germain.

8. Cerrutti 1881 - Italian Designer Wear

15, place de la Madeleine
01 47 42 10 78

W

M° Madeleine
Mon 11-19,
Tue-Sat 10-19
€€€

For details see the St-Germain.

9. Polo Ralph Lauren - American Designer Wear

2, place de la Madeleine   M° Madeleine
01 58 62 54 54   Mon 11-19, Tue-Sat 10.30-19
A C M W   €€€

Since 1968 when Ralph Lauren launched his menswear label, Polo, it has become one of the world's most famous and most wanted fashion labels. As much a marketing genius as a designer, his collections capture the all-American life-style, dressing every aspect of it, with the Wall Street suit, the Wyoming ranch jeans or the glam dress for Oscar Night. The design aesthetic that keeps the crowds coming is all about nostalgic elegance mixed with modern casual comfort.

10. Adolfo Dominguez - Spanish Men and Womenswear

24, rue Royale   M° Madeleine
01 44 58 96 10   Mon-Sat 10.00-19.00
A M W   €€

Adolpho Dominguez was among the first in a new generation of designers to inject a fresh approach into Spanish fashion, back in the 1980s. A big success in his home country, this was the first Spanish label to go public. His style is modern, functional and casual with a loose silhouette and natural fabrics. Take a special look at the leather pieces, they usually offer good value for money. *Also at: 4, rue la Vrillière (Étienne Marcel – Les Halles).*

11. Cerrutti 1881 - Italian Designer Wear

27, rue Royale   M° Concorde
01 53 30 18 72   Mon 11-19, Tue-Sat 10-19
M   €€€

For details see St-Germain.

12. Chanel - French Designer Shoes

25, rue Royale   M° Madeleine
01 44 51 92 93   Mon-Sat 10.00-19.00
W   €€€

This boutique only sells shoes. For details see St-Honoré.

13. Bon Point - Children's Clothes

15, rue Royale · · · · · · · · · · · · M° Concorde
01 47 42 52 63 · · · · · · · · · · · · Mon-Sat 10.00-19.00
C · · · · · · · · · · · · · · · · · · · €€

You'll find babies clothes in this shop. For details see Étienne Marcel-Les Halles.

14. Daniel Swarowski - Crystal Jewellery

7, rue Royale · · · · · · · · · · · · · M° Concorde
01 40 17 07 40 · · · · · · · · · · · · Mon-Sat 10.00-18.30
A · · · · · · · · · · · · · · · · · · · €€

This Austrian company is over one hundred years old. It has supplied all the French fashion houses with crystals for their couture outfits over the years. During the 1990s the label has become more visible in the fashion world, adding younger looks to the collection, and by collaborating with big brands like Adidas. The handmade crystals have a fabulous shimmer and they are the perfect way to add some affordable glamour to your outfit, be it a bracelet, necklace or evening bag.

15. Thierry Mugler - French Designer Wear

10, rue Boissy d'Anglas · · · · · · · M° Concorde
01 43 12 57 57 · · · · · · · · · · · · Mon-Sat 10.00-19.00
M W · · · · · · · · · · · · · · · · · · €€€

For details see St-Germain.

16. John Lobb - Classic Men's Footwear

23, rue Boissy d'Anglas · · · · · · · M° Concorde
01 42 65 24 45 · · · · · · · · · · · · Mon-Sat 10.30-19.00
M · · · · · · · · · · · · · · · · · · · €€€

For details see St-Germain.

17. Tartine et Chocolat - Children's Clothes

22, rue Boissy d'Anglas   M° Champs-Elysées-Clemenceau
01 40 17 09 03   Mon-Sat 10.00-19.00
C   €€

For details see the Étienne Marcel – Les Halles.

18. Missoni - Luxury Knitwear

1, rue du Fbg-St-Honoré   M° Concorde
01 44 51 96 96   Mon-Sat 10.00-19.00
A M W   €€€

There's a big chance that this Italian family-run fashion house is back in the era of greatness it experienced in the 1970s. Ottavio and Rosita Missoni's mulitcoloured knitwear, with the signature flecked flame dye effect, has changed little over the years, and has enjoyed and enduring popularity. Daughter Angela, who has been running the business since 1997 has taken the luxurious jet-set knitwear into a new century with daring but elegant folklore-inspired pieces that fit perfectly with the on-going fashion mode.

19. Gucci - Italian Designer Wear and Accessories

2, rue du Fbg St-Honoré   M° Concorde
01 44 94 14 70   Mon-Sat 10.00-19.00
A M W   €€€

It was in the mid-1990s that Gucci made it's now legendary trans-formation from being on the verge of ruin to being one of the most sought-after fashion labels. The man behind the turn-around, Tom Ford, is now one of the most powerful men in fashion, and Gucci is still in the limelight with its deluxe rock-chic fashion serving us sea-sonal must-haves. The Gucci woman "a little bit more obvious than the YSL woman" as Ford himself puts it in Vogue, for Winter 2002 once more takes on a rock n' roll attitude dressed in oh-so-skinny satin pants, a zigzag jacquard kimono jacket pulled in with a obi belt, and pointy ankle-strapped heels. This is the sleek flagship store. *Also at: 350, rue St-Honoré (accessories) (St-Honoré).*

20. Prada - Italian Designer Wear and Accessories

6, rue du Fbg St-Honoré   M° Concorde
01 58 18 63 30   Mon 11-19, Tue-Sat 10-19
A W   €€€

This shop opened early in the summer of 2002. Here you'll find womenswear, including Prada Sport, and accessories. For details see no 95 this chapter.

21. Stephane Kélian - Fashionable Shoes

5, rue du Fbg St-Honoré   M° Concorde
01 44 51 64 19   Mon-Sat 10.00-19.00
M W   €€€

For details see St-Germain.

22. Jaeger - British Designer Wear

5, rue du Fbg St-Honoré   M° Concorde
01 42 65 22 46   Mon-Sat 10.00-19.00
M W   €€€

When British designer Bella Freud, known for her quirky designs, was hired by Jaeger in the year of 2000 to vamp things up at the century-old label – a favourite of well-off country women - it seemed like a rather odd match; but the marriage has worked out perfectly. Freud's English sense of humour, urban coolness and her love of classic English fabrics like tweed, a Jaeger staple, gave the right injection. White trousers with a black stripe add rock' n ' roll flair to a tuxedo. A chiffon blouse gets hip with graphic stars, and a twinset is heated up with cartoon colours.

23. Sergio Rossi - Italian Fashionable Footwear

11, rue du Fbg-St-Honoré   M° Concorde
01 40 07 10 89   Mon-Sat 10.30-19.00
A W   €€€

For details see St-Germain.

24. Iceberg - Italian Fashion

12, rue du Fbg St-Honoré M° Concorde
01 40 06 00 89 Mon-Sat 11.00-19.00
M W €€€

The Italian label Iceberg, makes clothes with a youthful, easy and out-going attitude. Add to that graphic prints, body-emphasizing shapes, intense colours and the adverts with ironic-icon Pamela Anderson, and you've pretty much got the picture. Actually the clothes can be really flattering, even for those who aren't Baywatch babes.

25. Lolita Lempicka - Fanciful Designer Wear

14, rue du Fbg St-Honoré M° Concorde
01 49 24 94 01 Mon-Sat 10.30-19.00
W €€€

Most people come here for the evening wear. Long dresses are strap-less or backless and comes with lace, embroidery, feathers or beads in varying degrees, all for maximum impact when making grand party entrances. The day dresses are in a romantic forties mood. Not for everybody, but it's personality rather than age that determines if Lempicka will work out for you. *Also at: 78, avenue Marceau, 46, avenue Victor Hugo (Passy – Victor Hugo).*

26. Camper - Casual Footwear

14-16, rue du Fbg St-Honoré M° Concorde
01 42 68 13 65 Mon-Sat 10.00-19.00
M W €€

The shoes from Majorcan company, Camper are inexpensive, simple and comfortable, with that extra something that catches the eye. Some styles are inspired by Majorcan farmer's footwear, others have cushioned rubber soles. Perhaps best known are the asymmetrical "Twins", a pair of shoes that are alike but never the same. This is the concept-store - the interior changes every couple of month. *Also at: 9, rue des Francs Bourgeois (Le Marais), 1, rue du Cherche-Midi (St-Germain), 55, rue de Passy (Passy – Victor Hugo).*

27. Bottega Veneta - Italian Leather Goods and Clothes

16, rue Fbg St-Honoré   M° Concorde
01 42 65 59 70   Mon-Sat 10.00-19.00
A M W   €€€

The Italian leather goods house, Bottega Veneta, has earned an almost cult-like status with its really exclusive (and expensive) bags and accessories. Its signature woven leather Intrecciato line is a must-have for every style aficionado. In 2001 the Gucci group bought the label, and Tomas Ma er was made new creative director. Until now the clothes haven't been available in Paris, but this new boutique stocks men's and womenswear as well as the cool new accessories line for men.

28. Lanvin - French Designer Wear

15, rue du Fbg St-Honoré   M° Concorde
01 44 71 33 33   Mon-Sat 10.00-18.45
M   €€€

This shop sells menswear. For details see no 30.

29. La Perla - Italian Lingerie

20, rue du Fbg St-Honoré   M° Concorde
01 43 12 33 60   Mon-Sat 10.30-19.00
L   €€€

For details see St-Germain.

30. Lanvin - French Designer Wear

22, rue du Fbg St-Honoré   M° Concorde
01 44 71 31 83   Mon-Sat 10.00-18.45
W   €€€

Watch this space! Designer Alber Elbaz who was kicked out of YSL when Gucci bought the label, has now turned up at this classic French house. His first collection indicates a comeback with an urban, understated chic look in muted colours. He delivers a luxurious compromise between the feminine and the vicious as seen in overcoats and pantsuits. *Also at: 52, rue Bonaparte (St-Germain), 15 rue Fbg St-Honoré (men), 32, rue Marbeuf (this chapter).*

31. Gianfranco Ferré - Italian Designer Fashion

23, rue du Fbg St-Honoré   M° Concorde
01 42 66 69 30   Mon-Sat 10.30-19.30
M   €€€

You'll find menswear here. For details see the av George V entry.

32. Hermès - French Luxury Leather House

24, rue du Fbg St-Honoré   M° Concorde
01 40 17 47 17   Mon-Sat 10.00-19.00
A M W   €€€

Hermès isn't the first old bourgeois brand to have transformed itself and become desirably hip. But for many, as well as the luxury industry itself, Hermès with its low-key coolness is the reference point. The reputation is built on the icon handbags, as highly coveted today as in the mid-20th century when Grace Kelly carried the Kelly bag or Jackie O dangled her "Constance". They remain the ultimate in quality with higher than high prices. Add to that a waiting list of 6 months for the most-wanted ones. Avant-garde designer Martin Margiela does the elegant ready-to-wear range with long-lined silhouettes for classy women. Véronique Nichanian creates the posh men's line. This is the best Paris store, worth a visit just for people-watching, if nothing else.

33. Valentino - Italian Couturier

27, rue du Fbg St-Honoré   M° Concorde
01 42 66 95 94   Mon-Sat 10.00-19.00
M W   €€€

For details see no 105 this chapter.

34. Givenchy - French Couturier

28, rue du Fbg St-Honoré   M° Concorde
01 42 65 54 54   Mon-Sat 10.00-19.00
A M W   €€€

For details see no 72 this chapter.

35. Yves St-Laurent - French Designer

38, rue du Fbg St-Honoré   M° Concorde
01 42 65 74 59   Mon 11-19,
                                  Tue-Sat 10.30-19
W   €€€

For further details see St-Germain.

36. Jitrois - Leather Fashion

40, rue du Fbg St.Honoré   M° Concorde
01 47 42 60 09   Mon-Sat 11.00-19.00
M W   €€€

Jean-Claude Jitrois is famous for his jet-set chic leather clothes. The leathers are ultra-soft and the body-sculpturing designs have all the head-turning details that glamour kittens want. He works with metallic shades and strong colours. And his innovative high-tech fabrics such as stretch leather, make it possible for a pair of trousers to keep their original shape without sagging at the knees or the behind. Expect to pay €950 for a pair of leather jeans.

37. Apostrophe – Elegant French Fashion

43, rue du Fbg St-Honoré   M° Concorde
01 40 06 91 60   Mon-Sat 10.00-19.00
W   €€

Grown-up, elegant but restrained fashion-aware clothes sum up what Apostrophe stands for. If you're in your thirties and want a career look that's easy-to-wear yet stylish, this is for you. A sombre colour palette and flattering lines come in key pieces, such as urban modern trousers, sensual leather jackets and cashmere sweaters. Good value for money. *Also at: 1, rue du Boccador, 23, rue de Cambon (St-Honoré), 1 bis, place des Victoires (Étienne Marcel - Les Halles), 54, rue Bonaparte, 190, boulevard St-Germain (St-Germain), 5, avenue Victor Hugo (Passy - Victor Hugo).*

38. Christian Dior - French Couturier

46, rue du Fbg St-Honoré   M° Concorde
01 44 51 55 51   Mon-Sat 10.00-19.00
A W   €€€

For details see no 104 this chapter.

39. Leonard - French Designer Wear

48, rue du Fbg St-Honoré   M° Concorde
01 42 65 53 53   Mon-Sat 10.00-19.00
M W   €€€

In May 2001 Michele and Olivier Chatenet, the designer duo behind hotter-than-hot E2-label, was called in to vamp things up at the Leonard label. Since 1960 founder Daniel Triboullard has been creating beautiful silk jersey prints, untouched by the comings and goings of fashion. The Chatenet's respectful take on the Leonard heritage of floral patterns has been praised by the fashion-world, and is seen as a role-model for how to up date fashion labels. It's a cool remix with re-proportioned clothes, smooth colour combinations, and smart use of patterns like full-blown pink flowers on soft jersey dresses. *Also at: 36, avenue Pierre 1er de Serbie.*

40. Salvatore Ferragamo - Italian Shoes and Clothes

50, rue du Fbg St-Honoré   M° Concorde
01 43 12 96 96   Mon-Sat 11.00-19.00
A M W   €€€

See no 112 this chapter for details.

41. JP Tod's - Italian Shoes and Accessories

52, rue du Fbg St-Honoré   M° Concorde
01 42 66 66 65   Mon-Sat 10.30-19.00
A M W   €€€

For details see the St-Germain.

42. Comme des Garçons - Designer Wear

54, rue du Fbg St-Honoré   M° Concorde
01 53 30 27 27   Mon-Sat 11.00-19.00
M W   €€€

After her first catwalk show in Paris in 1981 Rei Kawakubo was hugely influential in changing the way clothes were seen in the 1980s. Her conceptual clothes are more inspired by the Japanese than the European clothing tradition. Her level of cutting and the fabrics are truly innovative. Every season she changes register, but still succeeds in retaining her unique identity. The label is a huge success, her annual turnover double that of Yamamoto or Miyake. The boutique is worth a visit for the spectacular interior, with varying shades of red fibreglass designed by Kawakubo herself and architect Takao Kawasaki. You also find the less expensive label, Comme des Garçons Comme des Garçons, and some clothes by her brilliant assistant Junya Watanabe.

43. Chloé - French Designer Wear

56, rue du Fbg St-Honoré   M° Concorde
01 44 94 33 00   Mon-Sat 10.00-19.00
W   €€€

When Stella McCartney left Chloé after four successful years for her own new label early in 2001, it came as a surprise, even for fashion insiders that 27-year old Phoebe Philo, McCartney's design assistant, had been chosen for the prestigious task of replacing her. After a few seasons there is no doubt she was the woman for the job, keeping the sexy celebrity rock-chic style that was McCartney's winning formula, but adding her own personal taste and a strong street sensibility.

44. Versace - Italian Designer Fashion

62, rue du Fbg St-Honoré   M° Concorde
01 47 42 88 02   Mon 11-19,
    Tue-Sat 10-19

A M W   €€€

Gianni Versace was the sole king of rock'n roll fashion, dressing rock-stars and royals who wanted the most attention-grabbing outfits. With extravagant colours, prints and sirocco-hot sexiness, he brought Hollywood glamour back into fashion. After his death in 1997, his sister and muse Donatella succeeded him, and she has stayed true to his design principles, adding her own sense of what women want to wear. The Fbg St-Honoré store seems to be built on the "more is more principle", both style- and size-wise. Besides the women and menswear, there is also a cosmetic range, luggage and the home collection. *Also at: 41, rue Francois 1er.*

45. Etro - Italian Designer Wear

66, rue du Fbg St-Honoré   M° Concorde
01 40 07 09 40   Mon-Sat 10-13-14-19
A M W   €€€

For details see St-Germain.

46. Roberto Cavalli - Italian Designer Wear

68, rue du Fbg St-Honoré   M° Concorde
01 44 94 04 15   Mon-Sat 10.00-19.30
A M W   €€€

Roberto Cavalli is the Bacchus of Italian fashion. He designs party-starter clothes for the rock-star or wannabe that wishes to outline her personal assets. Attractions are the higher than high heels, dangerously curvaceous silhouettes, exotic animal prints and ostentatious materials such as fur, leather and snakeskin. For Winter 2002/3 the Cavalli girl becomes a lady with a brown patent leather suit, leopard print coat, brocade jeans and a white fur floor-trailing parka.

47. Sonia Rykiel - French Designer

70, rue du Fbg Saint-Honoré   M° Madeleine
01 42 65 20 81   Mon-Sat 10.30-19.45
A W   €€€

Further details see the St-Germain.

48. John Galliano - Designer Fashion

84, rue du Fbg-St-Honoré   M° Champs-Elysées-Clemenceau
W   €€€

John Galliano opens his first Parisian own-label boutique in October 2002. The collections are very similar to what he creates for Dior. For further information see Dior at avenue Montaigne.

49. Christian Lacroix - French Couturier

73, rue du Fbg St-Honoré   M° Concorde
01 42 68 79 04   Mon-Sat 10.00-19.00
C W   €€€

Ever since his debut collection in 1987 put a new spin on the couture stage, Lacroix has had his cult devotees all over the world. He's the master of colour and print with a strong flair for the theatrical and baroque. Rather than full-on sexuality, his creations stand for dashing romance with asymmetrical lines, flounces en masse, textural mixes and fairytale decoration. Southern France is a source of inspiration. Besides his ready-to-wear collection you'll find his second line, Bazar, and a new line for girls aged 4-16 years.

50. Walter Steiger - Modern Footwear

83, rue du Fbg St-Honoré   M° Champs-Elysées-Clemenceau
01 42 66 44 68   Mon-Sat 11.00-19.00
M W   €€

Swiss-born Walter Steiger is famous for his highly innovative and sophisticated shoe constructions, and has been in demand by several couturiers like Chanel, Karl Lagerfeld and Chloé. The look is classic, sometimes with retro-glam influences. He also does a lot of modern-looking loafers, ankle boots and ballerinas that are really comfortable – perfect for exploring the asphalt jungle by foot. *Also at: 183, boulevard St Germain (St-Germain).*

51. Tartine et Chocolat – Children's Clothes

105, rue du Fbg St-Honoré   M° Champs-Elysées-Clemenceau
01 45 62 44 04   Mon-Sat 10.00-19.00
C   €€

For details see the Étienne Marcel - Les Halles.

52. Hugo Boss - Modern Men and Womenswear

12, rd pnt des Champs Elysées   M° Franklin-D.Roosevelt
01 45 62 57 57   Mon-Sat 10.00-19.30
A M W   €€

Hugo Boss has built its multinational success on good quality menswear, synonymous with power-lunch suits; a well-tailored look with quality fabrics at reasonable prices. The 2002 men's collection has taken a new path, with clothes that seem more on speaking terms with Helmut Lang than the label's own past. It's a modern fresh look with clean silhouettes and sharp cuts that Lothar Reiff, the creative director, has put forward. Hugo for both men and women is the youngest line with a sporty attitude. This is the Parisian flagship store. *Also at: 374, rue Saint-Honoré, 165, rue Saint-Honoré (Hugo), 352, rue Saint-Honoré (Boss Sport), 34, avenue de l'Opéra (Boss Women), 43, avenue de l'Opéra (Opéra), 19, rue l'Ancienne Comédie (St-Germain).*

53. L'Eclaireur - International Designer Wear

26, avenue des Champs Elysées   M° Franklin-D.Roosevelt
01 45 62 12 32   Mon-Sat 11.00-19.00
A M W   €€€

For details see Le Marais.

54. Stephane Kélian - Fashionable Shoes

26, avenue des Champs Elysées M° Franklin-D.Roosevelt
01 42 56 42 26   Mon-Sat 10.00-19.00
W   €€€

For details see St-Germain.

55. Zara - Spanish High-Street Fashion

38-40, avenue des Ch. Elysées   M° Franklin-D.Roosevelt
01 56 59 97 10   Mon-Sat 10.00-22.00
A C M W   €

For details see Étienne Marcel – Les Halles.

56. Guerlain - Scent

68, avenue des Champs Elysées   M° Franklin-D.Roosevelt
01 45 62 52 57   Mon-Sat 09.45-19.00
B   €€€

This, the original Guerlain boutique, is one of the last reminders of
the Champs-Elysées' golden age. Today the former family-run company is owned by LVMH, but you can still buy the wonderful classic
Guerlain fragrances here. These wonderful and seductive scents, like
Vol de Nuit and for men Habit Rouge offer something completely
different from what the company's newer scents are about and some
are only available here.

57. Sephora - Beauty Megastore

70, avenue des Champs Elysées   M° Franklin-D.Roosevelt
01 53 93 22 50   Mon-Sat 10-24, Sun 12-24
B   €€

Department stores, beauty boutiques, and fragrance brands are
scrambling to catch up with the success of LVMH-owned Sephora,
whose department store concept specifically focused on beauty, is
turning the industry upside down. This enormous megastore car-

ries more than 12,000 products in every price range, and you can touch and smell everything without involving any pushy salesperson. They also sell Sephora's own-brand products. Sephora Blanc is the concept-store located at the charming Cour St-Emilon in the 12th arr, which carries smaller, and more hard-to-find brands. They also stock products for holistic well-being. *Also at: Forum des Halles (Étienne Marcel - Les Halles).*

58. Tara Jarmon - Modern Womenswear

73, avenue des Champs Elysées M° George V
01 45 63 45 41   Mon-Sat 10.30-19.00
W   €€

For details see St-Germain.

59. Furla - Italian Leather Accessories and Shoes

74, avenue des Champs Elysées M° Franklin-D.Roosevelt
01 40 75 02 40   Mon-Sat 10.00-19.00
A W   €€

The Bologna-based leather house Furla, founded in 1927, is an international success with boutiques all over the world. The design is safe but sleek, urban chic in the typical Italian way, at much more affordable prices than the top prestigious leather houses. *Also at: 8, rue de Sèvres (St-Germain).*

60. Etam - High-Street Womenswear

84, avenue des Champs Elysées M° George V
01 45 61 28 09   Mon-Sat 10.00-19.00
C L W   €

For details see St-Honoré.

61. Lacoste - French Sports and Leisurewear

95, avenue des Champs Elysées M° George V
01 47 23 76 00   Mon-Sat 10.00-19.00
M W   €€

French tennis player René Lacoste, nick-named "the crocodile", launched his first polo shirt in 1933, the first example of sportswear as fashion. Since then the crocodile has been seen on every kind of sports and leisurewear, all over the world. In 2001 designer Christopher Lemaire was brought in for a much needed face-lift. He has worked for YSL and Lacroix, and his first promising collections draw from the label's heritage of sporty elegance but is made modern with clean lines and silhouettes. Think 1950s Riviera. *Also at: 37, bd des Capucines (Opéra), 161, bd St-Germain (St-Germain), 70-72, rue du Fbg St-Antoine (Other Destinations).*

62. Louis Vuitton - French Luxury Leather and Clothes

101, av. des Champs Elysées   M° George V
01 53 57 24 00   Mon-Sat 10.00-20.00
A M W   €€€

Ever since it was created in 1886 the LV monogram has been one of the world's most perennial status symbols, and there is probably no other logo that has spawned as many rip-offs. Since 1996 American designer Marc Jacobs has turned the predictable bourgeois brand into the ultimate urban cool. Jacobs, who once took grunge to the catwalk, has taken his understated nonchalant bohemian aesthetic, and fused it with luxury sensibility and lean 1970s vibes, creating an effortless jet-set sexy look. The equally gorgeous bags and shoes add to the magic. Winter 2002/3 the look is of discreet charm and luxury, and the little metallic mesh shoulder bag is this season's quiet, yet undisputed monogram statement. This is the only Paris store that sells the ready-to-wear clothes. *Also at: 54, Avenue Montaigne and 6, pl. St-Germain-des-Près (St-Germain).*

63. Petit Bateau – Children's Clothes and Women's t-shirts

116, av. des Champs Elysées   M° George V
01 40 74 02 03   Mon 10-19.30, Tue-Sat 10-20
C W   €

For details see St-Germain.

64. Bally - Urban Chic

146, av. des Champs Elysées   M° George V
01 44 13 87 70   Mon-Sat 10.00-19.30
A M W   €€€

For details see Opéra.

65. Hermès - French Luxury Leather House

42, avenue George V   M° George V
01 47 20 48 51   Mon-Sat 10.00-18.00
A M W   €€€

For details see no 32 this chapter.

66. Armani Collezioni - Italian Designer Wear

41, avenue George V   M° George V
01 56 89 06 50   Mon-Sat 10.00-19.30
A M W   €€€

This newly-opened thousand square metres shop, on two levels
houses Armani's Collezioni line, priced between top-label Giorgio
Armani and diffusion line Emporio Armani.

67. Morabito - French Leather Goods House

40, avenue George V   M° George V
01 53 23 90 40   Mon-Fri 10-18.45, Sat 11-18.30
A   €€€

For details see St-Honoré.

68. Gianfranco Ferré - Italian Designer Fashion

38 bis, 44 avenue George V   M° George V
01 53 57 67 01   Mon-Sat 10.30-19.30
M W   €€€

That Milan-based designer Gianfranco Ferré started out as an architect probably explains why his designs have been characterised by
clean architectural lines and a dramatic play with proportions. He
started his own ready-to-wear line in 1978, and for a while he designed haute couture for Dior. His clothes for the self-assured diva
always follow in the tradition of elegance and glamour, as seen in his
signature white shirts with precision tailoring and an exaggeration
of detail. He usually works with neutral colours and dashes of his
signature red. *Also at: 23, rue du Fbg St-Honoré (men).*

69. JEY Store - International Designer Wear

38, avenue George V   M° George V
01 53 57 67 00   Mon-Sat 10.00-19.30
M W   €€€

The plush newly-opened 1,000 square metres JEY store houses a cool
mix of international designers. They are the only Paris stockist of
American designers Anna Sui and Michael Kors signature line, and
Italian Bluemarine, designed by Anna Molinari. Other hot labels are
Alexander McQueen, Roberto Cavalli, Dirk Bikkemberg and Martine
Sitbon.

70. Kenzo - Designer Wear

18, avenue George V   M° George V
01 47 23 33 49   Mon-Sat 10.00-19.00
A W   €€€

For details see St-Germain.

71. Balenciaga - Cutting-edge Designer Wear

10, avenue George V   M° Alma-Marceau
01 47 20 21 11   Mon-Sat 10.00-19.00
A W   €€€

When Nicolas Ghesquière took over this venerable Spanish fashion house in 1997 he was unknown. Today he is one of the most influential designers, able to change the look of the season with one outfit. The sexy hard-edge chic seen in his coveted collections is characterized by his expert cuts, silhouettes that contrast with the fabrics, and a 1980s flavour. Ghesquière proves that avant-garde fashion is not only fun but wearable as well. Be sure to check out the to-die-for accessories and don't leave without a pair of the sexy-cut trousers. This store, the only one in Paris, is on the site of Balenciaga's original couture house.

72. Givenchy - French Couturier

3,8, avenue George V   M° George V
01 44 31 51 25   Mon-Sat 10.00-19.00
A M W   €€€

It was in 1952 that Hubert de Givenchy set up his own haute couture house. With Audrey Hepburn as his muse, he created clothes with daring elegance and simplicity in design. When he retired in 1995 first Galliano, then Alexander McQueen followed. In 2001 Julien McDonald was commissioned to give Givenchy that new identity it sought so eagerly. Only 30 years old, he is the youngest designer working in haute couture. He does women's ready-to-wear as well, but after two seasons he is still searching for the winning formula. The knitwear, his original claim to fame, is the best bet. He doesn't handle the men's line that is simply fine tailoring with modern attitude. The Vision label is the cheaper women's line. *Also at 28, rue du Fbg St-Honoré; 56, rue Francois 1er (this chapter); 5, rue du Cherche-Midi (accessories) (St-Germain)*

73. Cerrutti 1881 - Italian Designer Wear

48, rue Pierre Charron   M° George V
01 40 70 18 81   Mon 11-19, Tue-Sat 10-19
M   €€€

For details see St-Germain.

74. Agnès b. - French Casual Chic

17, 25, av. Pierre-1er-de-Serbie   M° Iéna
01 47 20 22 44   Mon-Sat 10.00-19.00
M W   €€

At No. 25 you'll find a menswear store. For details see St-Honoré.

75. Leonard – French Designer Wear

36, avenue Pierre 1er de Serbie   M° Iéna
01 53 67 87 66   Mon-Sat 10.00-19.00
M W   €€€

For details see no 39 this chapter.

76. Marcel Lassance - Relaxed Menswear

21, rue Marbeuf   M° Franklin-D.Roosevelt
01 49 52 09 01   Mon-Sat 10.00-19.00
M   €€€

For more details, see St-Germain.

77. Berluti - Elegant Men's Shoes

26, rue Marbeuf   M° Alma-Marceau
01 43 59 51 10   Mon-Sat 10.00-19.00
M W   €€€

Berluti's handcrafted men's shoes are a favourite of the concerning elite around the world. Founded in 1885 by Alessandro Berluti, the family business was bought by LVMH in 1993. It's still run by a

member of the family, Olga Berluti, who sticks to the winning formula with top quality ready-to-wear and custom-made shoes in the
most exquisite materials. To keep the style modern and original she
has developed new lines in tune with the times. There is also a small
collection of women's shoes.

78. Lanvin – French Designer Wear

32, rue Marbeuf	M° Franklin-D.Roosevelt
01 53 75 02 20	Mon-Sat 10.00-19.00
W	€€€

For details see no 30 this chapter.

79. Givenchy - French Couturier

56, rue Francois 1er	M° Franklin-D.Roosevelt
01 40 76 00 21	Mon-Sat 10.00-19.00
M	€€€

This shop sells menswear. For no 72 this chapter.

80. Morabito - French leather Goods House

55, rue Francois 1er	M° Franklin-D.Roosevelt
01 53 23 90 40	Mon-Fri 10-18.45, Sat 11-18.30
A	€€€

Morabito is another French leather goods house, not as well-known
as the other luxury heavy-weights. The company that was founded
in 1905 by Jean-Baptiste Morabito makes handbags in low-key elegant styles. Unaffected by fashion and trends there is a timeless quality to the clean beautiful shapes as seen in the latest Boulogne-line.
They also do made-to-measure. *Also at: 40, avenue George V.*

81. John Lobb - Classic Men's Footwear

51, rue Francois 1er	M° Franklin-D.Roosevelt
01 45 61 02 55	Mon-Sat 10.30-19.00
M	€€€

For details see St-Germain.

82. Ermenegildo Zegna - Italian Tailoring

48 bis, rue Francois 1er	M° Franklin-D.Roosevelt
01 56 89 14 00	Mon-Sat 10.00-19.00
M	€€€

The Zegna trademark is classic tailoring in rich and supple fabrics with obsessive attention to detail. Many refer to it as the "Rolls Royce" of menswear and celebs such as John Travolta and Hugh Grant wear Zegna suits. The family-run business with an artisan spirit was founded in the early 1900s. Whether you go for the Napoli Couture line or the ready-to-wear selection you get clothes with a self-assured understated elegance. Today's collections draw inspiration from the 1950 and 60s, with a modern lightness and innovative fabrics, which also holds for the high-tech sports line. *Also at: 368, rue St-Honoré (St-Honoré), 10, rue de la Paix (Opéra).*

83. Paule Ka - Modern Chic Womenswear

45, rue Francois 1er	M° Franklin-D.Roosevelt
01 47 20 76 10	Mon-Sat 10.00-19.00
W	€€€

This is not for the fashion-victim. Serge Cajfinger dresses modern women who like clothes that are timeless, classic and sexy at the same time. Think Audrey Hepburn-chic. The style is truly Parisian – both practical and alluring, you have the complete look here, from the office to the Oscars. *Also at: 192, boulevard St-Germain (St-Germain), 20, rue Mahler (Le Marais).*

84. Francesco Smalto - Tailored Menswear

44, rue Francois 1er   M° Franklin-D.Roosevelt
01 47 20 70 63   Mon-Sat 10.00-19.00
M   €€€

Elegantly tailored suits are Francesco Smalto's trademark. Either go
for the couture where you get serious suits and shirts that fit perfectly
in a couple of weeks; or take the ready-to-wear option. There is also
more relaxed clothing such as colourful party suits, leather jackets and
casual trousers. *Also at: 5, place Victor Hugo (Passy - Victor Hugo).*

85. Versace - Italian Designer Fashion

41, rue Francois 1er   M° Franklin-D.Roosevelt
01 47 23 88 30   Mon 11-19, Tue-Sat 10-19
M W   €€€

For details see the rue du Fbg St-Honoré entry.

86. Courrèges - French Designer Wear

40, rue Francois 1er   M° Franklin-D.Roosevelt
01 53 67 30 73   Mon-Sat 10.00-19.00
A W   €€€

Though the label recently celebrated its 40th anniversary, there is no
sign of mid-life crisis at Courrèges. On the contrary, the ultra-modern
look is as fresh as ever. Vintage pieces such as cute space-age dresses,
logo ribbed-knits and boots are hot collectors items and big designer labels draw inspiration from André and Coqueline Courrèges'
graphic minidresses and flat calf-length boots. At the flagship store
you'll find a vast range of the now iconic designs, as well as accessories and the T-bar shoes - Rei Kawakubo's favourite.

87. Balmain - French Couturier

35,44, rue Francois 1er   M° Franklin-D.Roosevelt
01 56 89 16 00   Mon-Sat 10.00-19.00
W   €€€

Now that designer Oscar de la Renta is leaving the couture business, staid Balmain is in search of a new identity. New ready-to-wear designer is French Laurent Mercier. He started out on the wild side, creating stage outfits for rock star Lenny Kravitz, but is famous in Paris fashion circles as a former star of the drag-queen scene. For his debut collection Winter 2002/3 he showed sharp tailoring, blended with kimono-inspired lounge wear drawing from the style of the 1920s – aviator and kimono-wrap jackets, and chiffon pyjamas with wide pants under knit cardigans.

88. Fendi - Italian Designer Accessories and Clothes

24, rue Francois 1er	M° George V
01 49 52 84 52	Mon-Sat 10.00-19.00
A M W	€€€

One of the period-defining must-have bags, the Fendi baguette brought the Italian family-run company back to the top in the late 1990s. However, it wasn't until 2001 that the Parisians got their 600 square-metre flagship store. Here sophisticated Fendi jet-set glamour reigns, and on the first floor all the to-die-for accessories are lined up, ready to be snapped up by fashion editors. On the second floor find more baguettes, luggage and Karl Lagerfeld's gorgeous clothes for men and women that have all the sex appeal you could want. And here, in the VIP salon, are the fabulous furs, the Fendi sisters' original claim to fame.

89. Thomas Pink - Classic Shirts

19, rue Francois 1er	M° George V
01 47 23 72 00	Mon-Sat 10.00-19.00
M W	€€

It's a little-known fact that the phrase "in the pink" was inspired by Thomas Pink. This legendary Mayfair tailor made his name in the late 18th century, creating hunting coats that were regarded as the finest in the UK. His high quality standards live on at the company, which today mainly sells well-made and well-priced shirts. The extensive range includes both men and women's shirts that follow the classic British tailoring traditions. The fashion factor has risen lately, the black shirt was a winner as was the ruffled shirt for women. And, with the new box-shaped women's shirt "Hepburn" as well as the Slimfit with a deep collar, there is surely something shirty going on.

90. Scarlett - Vintage Designer Clothes and Accessories

10, rue Clement Marot   M° Franklin-D.Roosevelt
01 56 89 03 00   Mon-Fri 11-19.30, Sat 14-19
A W   €€€

Check this place out if you are searching for yet another item for your vintage collection. The small boutique is jam-packed with items from all classical fashion houses, be it Pucci, Hèrmes, Courrèges or Chanel. Every thing is in good condition, and prices are what you would expect when you're into expensive habits like this.

91. Camerlo - Designer Wear

4, rue de Marignan   M° Franklin-D.Roosevelt
01 47 23 77 06   Mon-Sat 10.30-19.30
A W   €€€

Dany Camerlo's multi-label store draws an urban chic clientele that wants eye-catching clothes from labels like Laurent Mercier or Versace. If you want a more low-key look, go for Alberta Ferretti or Van der Straeten. For accessories, find cool shoes from Bruno Frisoni.

92. Apostrophe - Elegant French Fashion

1, rue du Boccador   M° Franklin-D.Roosevelt
01 56 89 20 80   Mon-Sat 10.00-19.00
W   €€

For information see no 37 this chapter.

93. Plein Sud – Trendy Womenswear

2, avenue Montaigne   M° Alma-Marceau
01 47 20 42 43   Mon-Sat 10.00-19.30
W   €€

In September 2002 Plein-Sud opened this new flag-ship store. For details see Étienne Marcel - Les Halles.

94. Emanuel Ungaro - French Couturier

2, avenue Montaigne   M° Alma-Marceau
01 53 57 00 00   Mon-Sat 10.00-19.00
A W   €€€

Things have hotted up considerably here over the last few years. Ungaro, who started his couture house in 1965, has always created feminine clothes using delicate fabrics and surface detail; and trained as he was by Balenciaga, always with a sharp sense of cut. In 2001 Giambattista Valli was brought in to attract a younger, hipper clientele. He now designs the ready-to-wear range (Ungaro still does the couture) and it seems that he has caught some of the master's magic. While still being faithful to the label's tradition, he has given it street-cred with a sensual romanticism mixed with a bit of rock-chic. *Also at: 33, rue de Grenelle; this shop stocks accessories, and the luxurious interior is created by Antonio Citterio.*

95. Prada - Italian Designer Wear and Accessories

10, avenue Montaigne   M° Alma-Marceau
01 53 23 99 40   Mon-Sat 10.00-19.00
A M W   €€€

Prada, needs no further introduction, it's been at the front line of fashion since its nylon bags became the hottest accessories in the mid 1990s. Fashion house designer Miuccia Prada's collections always succeed in combining her own unique statement with some of the season's hottest trends and must-have items. This is the largest store in Paris and the only one that sells menswear. *Also at: 6, rue Fbg de St-Honoré (no 20 this chapter); 3-9, rue de Grenelle, (St-Germain).*

181

96. Malo - Luxury Italian Cashmere

12, avenue Montaigne	M° Franklin-D.Roosevelt
01 47 20 26 08	Mon-Sat 10.00-19.00
M W	€€€

Looking for that deluxe cashmere piece that will last a lifetime? Then Malo is the place. With this top Italian cashmere master it's all about expensive sweaters. The look is classic but with a fashion or sporty twist that gives the polos, V-necks, cardigans and sweatshirts that little something extra. Everything is made in Tuscany and finished by hand. Prices definitely demand that you see your purchase as a long-term investment.

97. Bon Point - Children's Clothes

12, avenue Montaigne	M° Franklin-D.Roosevelt
01 47 20 42 10	Mon-Sat 10.00-19.00
C	€€

For details see the Étienne Marcel – Les Halles.

98. Inés de la Fressange - Classic-chic Womenswear

14, avenue Montaigne	M° Franklin-D.Roosevelt
01 47 23 08 94	Mon-Sat 10.00-19.00
W	€€€

Former model, and the face of Chanel in the 1980s, Inès de la Fressange is to many the quintessential Parisian woman. Her "clothing solutions" respond to the modern woman's needs with wardrobe essentials of impeccable quality. The look is made up of Kathrine Hepburnesque basics in a variety of silhouettes to suit women of different sizes and ages.

99. Joseph - Fashionable Womenswear

14, avenue Montaigne   M° Franklin-D.Roosevelt
01 47 20 39 55   Mon-Sat 10.30-19.00
W   €€

For details see St-Honoré.

100. Regina Rubens - Classic Womenswear

16, avenue Montaigne   M° Alma-Marceau
01 47 20 32 32   Mon-Sat 10.00-19.00
W   €€

Regina Rubens makes no fuss real-life clothes. It's a classic sport-chic
look with reasonably priced basics such as suits and trousers. The
timeless clothes have a high comfort level, and as an extra service
they make clothes in smaller or larger sizes if needed – they cost 20
percent extra. It takes two weeks and they ship abroad at no extra
charge. *Also at: 15, rue Pavée; 182, boulevard St-Germain; 15, rue Passy.*

101. Montaigne 18 - Fashionable Furs

18, avenue Montaigne   M° Franklin-D.Roosevelt
01 47 20 43 43   Mon-Sat 10.00-19.00
W   €€€

When it comes to fashionable furs, Fendi ranks highest of them all.
Designed by Karl Lagerfeld, it was Fendi who bought fashion edge
into the world of fur, back in the 1960s. Today he still sets the tone
with cutting-edge cool designs and high-tech innovations.

102. Dolce & Gabbana - Italian Designer Fashion

22, avenue Montaigne   M° Alma-Marceau
01 42 25 68 78   Mon-Sat 10.00-19.30
A M W   €€€

For more than 20 years Italian design duo Domenico Dolce and Stefano Gabbana have been creating their sensual glam-rock clothes. Their devotion to the female form, Catholicism, 1940s screen stars and Sicilian-baroque have all been visible throughout the collections. The clothes come with sharp tailoring and gorgeous prints, and their suits cut with integral corsetry are famous. Their muse, Madonna, and other jet-set celebs are long-time devotees. The men's line is more pared-down, but with a strong Italian feeling. This 550 square metres flag-ship store was opened in July 2002.

103. Christian Lacroix - French Couturier

26, avenue Montaigne
01 47 20 68 95
C W

M° Franklin-D.Roosevelt
Mon-Sat 10.00-19.00
€€€

For details see no 49 this chapter.

104. Christian Dior - French Couturier

30, avenue Montaigne
01 40 73 54 44
A M W

M° Franklin-D.Roosevelt
Mon-Sat 10.00-19.00
€€€

Since 1996 John Galliano has re-built this old French fashion house, making it a must for every self-respecting fashion addict. His eclectic style, that no one else could pull off, is a daring mix of a trillion colours and prints, multi-ethnic references, bad boy streetwear, and feminine silhouettes, as seen in his brilliant bias-cut dresses. The accessories, crucial to every designer label, are simply gorgeous, like the coveted saddle-bag that is updated every season. Now that Heidi Slimane has joined forces to create the stunningly cool and elegant men's line, Dior is definitely scoring an all-time high. This is their huge boudoir-like flagship store, and the only one in Paris selling the menswear. *Also at: 46, rue du Fbg St-Honoré, 16 rue de l'Abbaye (St-Germain).*

105. Valentino - Italian Couturier

17-19   Avenue Montaigne   M° Alma-Marceau
01 47 23 64 61   Mon-Sat 10.00-19.00
A M W   €€€

The Italian design icon, Valentino, has been dressing the rich and famous since 1960 when he started his own business. Utterly elegant but with high-density glamour, his evening creations are for women with cleavages, curves and bottomless bank accounts. He also has the everyday look for the society lady as well as her daughter, may it be a Valentino-red dress, a slim smart suit, or trousers. For men the smoking jackets are movie-star gorgeous and the beautifully cut suits are just flawless. Miss V and O by Valentino are the second lines.

106. MaxMara - Italian Elegant Womenswear

31, avenue Montaigne   M° Franklin-D.Roosevelt
01 47 20 61 13   Mon-Sat 10.30-19.00
A W   €€

MaxMara bears all the signature marks that has made Italian fashion so popular: flattering cuts, clean lines, sober colours and high-quality fabrics at reasonable prices. The look is grown-up, effortless chic with beautiful clothes for work as well as evening. The company, one of Italy's largest, is famous for its discreet image. They use big-name designers, but exactly who they are is a well-kept secret. Look out for the brand new lingerie line. *Also at: 264, rue St-Honoré (St-Honoré); 37, rue du Four (St-Germain); 100, av Paul Doumer (Passy – Victor Hugo).*

107. Tika Tirawa - Sophisticated Knitwear

41, avenue Montaigne   M° Franklin-D.Roosevelt
01 56 62 35 35   Mon-Sat 10.00-19.00
W   €€

For details see St-Germain.

108. Emilio Pucci - Italian Designer Wear

36, avenue Montaigne   M° Alma Marceau
01 47 20 04 45   Mon-Sat 10.00-19.00
A M W   €€€

Few fashion features are as instantly recognisable as Pucci's swirling colourful prints, that perfectly summed up the psychedelic mood of the 1960s. Now that patterns are back in fashion, Italy's "Prints Charming" is once more inspiring the fashion industry. Adding to the buzz is the appointment of Christian Lacroix as new artistic director, and the opening of this new flagship store. So far Lacroix has declared that the heritage of the house must be respected, but injected with contemporary culture "everything from art and music to snowboarding" as he describes it to the Sunday Times. The Spring 2003 collection will show the transformation. Until then, you can't go wrong with a bit of Pucci power by the pool. Here you'll find men and womenswear.

109. Céline - French-American Chic

36, avenue Montaigne   M° Franklin-D.Roosevelt
01 56 89 07 92   Mon-Sat 10.00-19.00
A W   €€€

In 1997 the American designer Michael Kors was sent in to breathe new life into the prestigious but stodgy leather goods and ready-to wear house, Celine. He certainly made a remarkable turn around - for some years it was one of LVMH's fastest-growing fashion labels. The secret formula is that Kors knows exactly what his customers want. It is a sexy but risk-free take on American sportswear in luxurious fabrics with a hint of French chic as seen in cashmere turtlenecks, silk tank tops and leather trousers. *Also at: 58, rue de Rennes (St-Germain), 3, avenue Victor Hugo (Passy – Victor Hugo).*

110. Eres - Sophisticated Swimwear and Lingerie

40, avenue Montaigne
01 47 23 07 26
L W

M° Franklin-D.Roosevelt
Mon-Sat 10.00-19.00
€€€

For details see no 6 this chapter.

111. Chanel - French Designer Wear

42, avenue Montaigne
01 47 23 74 12
A W

M° Franklin-D.Roosevelt
Mon-Sat 10.00-19.00
€€€

For details see St-Honoré.

112. Salvatore Ferragamo - Italian Shoemaker

45, avenue Montaigne
01 47 23 36 37
A M W

M° Alma-Marceau
Mon-Sat 11.00-19.00
€€€

Salvatore Ferragamo is the person who during the first half of the last century, gave Italian shoes the reputation they enjoy today. Nowadays the Ferragamo dynasty also delivers other luxurious and elegant fashion items, although the leather goods are still the best choice. In 2002 Graeme Black, former Giorgio Armani designer, was called in to revamp their clothing line. Time will tell what that might bring. *Also at: 68/70, Rue des St-Pères (St-Germain) 50, rue du Fbg St-Honoré.*

113. Thierry Mugler - French Designer Wear

49, avenue Montaigne
01 47 23 37 62
M W

M° Franklin-D.Roosevelt
Mon-Sat 10.00-19.00
€€€

For details see St-Germain.

114. 51 Montaigne - Italian Designer Labels

51, avenue Montaigne
01 43 59 05 32
W

M° Franklin-D.Roosevelt
Mon-Sat 10.00-19.30
€€€

For a bit of dolce vita label glam this store is right on target, with a bunch of Italian labels such as Roberto Cavalli, Sergio Rossi, D&G, and Moschino. You can also pick up items from non-Italians like Vivienne Westwood and Lawrence Steel - still with that dazzle-factor. Add a tan and you have the perfect party-starter look.

115. Calvin Klein - American Designer Wear

53, avenue Montaigne
01 56 88 12 12
A B M O W

M° Franklin-D.Roosevelt
Mon-Sat 10.00-19.00
€€€

Calvin Klein is admired for being one of the designers most in tune with the zeitgeist, always knowing what the modern woman wants to wear. His clothes and his legendary ad campaigns display his urban cool minimalist aesthetic. He creates beautiful feminine clothes with a sly sexiness to them. Key features are his sophisticated takes on sportswear and men's tailoring, and his use of natural fabrics and colours. This brand new flagship store is the first in Europe, designed by British minimalist architect John Pawson. Here you find the men and women's line as well as the homeware - just about as minimalist as it can get.

116. Marni - Italian Designer Wear

57, avenue Montaigne
01 56 88 08 08
A W

M° Franklin-D.Roosevelt
Mon-Sat 10.00-19.00
€€€

Italian designer Consuelo Castiglioni's bourgeois bohemian blend of vintage-styled fabrics remixed in a somewhat whimsical way has been a huge trendsetter for a couple of years. A pair of loose-fitting striped trousers combined with a floral-print lace skirt and a coat in soft muted colours is typical of the Marni-look. Her over-sized accessories go well with the look giving it an extra edge. This flagship store opened in January 2002.

117. Loewe - Spanish Leather Goods House

46, avenue Montaigne   M° Franklin-D.Roosevelt
01 53 57 92 50   Mon-Sat 10.00-19.00
A W   €€€

Madrid-based leather goods house, Loewe recently appointed the avant-garde Belgian Jose Enrique Selfa as womenswear designer. The company, founded in 1846, now owned by LVMH, has been more about craft and tradition than trendiness. But with Selfa the hope is to heat things up a bit, and his first collection was a good start, especially the knitwear and his play on the house's leather tradition with hourglass-shaped leather dresses. The supply of deluxe accessories ensures that the jet-set clientele will come back for more.

118. Krizia - Italian Designer Wear

48, avenue Montaigne   M° Franklin-D.Roosevelt
01 47 20 25 02   Mon-Sat 10.00-19.00
W   €€€

Mariuccia Mandelli is the designer behind the Italian label Krizia. She started in the 1950s, and is still head of the design department (although Alber Elbaz and Jean-Paul Knott made short visits as artistic directors). Her clothes, that appeal to more mature women, have a flowing silhouette and often come with soft drapery. She uses luxury fabrics and the textures are often brilliant. Knitwear is a speciality.

119. Barbara Bui - Trendy Men and Womenswear

50, avenue Montaigne   M° Franklin-D.Roosevelt
01 42 25 05 25   Mon-Sat 10.00-19.00
A M W   €€

French-Vietnamese Barbara Bui does modern, wearable clothes in
tune with the trends of the season. The look is clean, urban elegance
with a hint of an edgier flavour to it. Modern fabrics and colours stay
in the neutral palette, and the trousers especially are always well cut
and comes in many different styles. The less expensive line, Barbara
Bui Initials, contains wardrobe basics. There is also a menswear line.
Also in: Étienne Marcel - Les Halles, Le Marais, St-Germain.

120. Jil Sander - Designer Wear

52, avenue Montaigne   M° Franklin-D.Roosevelt
01 44 95 06 70   Mon-Sat 10.00-19.00
A M W   €€€

To avid fashion-followers the name Jil Sander has come to epitomize
understated clothes with an androgynous sensuality to them and
the ultimate fit and quality. Not long after Prada's acquisition of the
company Sander herself left, and Milan Vukmirovic took her place
in the design seat. You still find the androgynous lines and sober
self-confident style, but Vukmorovic's straight-forward approach has
also brought in more colours and new materials. He has also elimina-
ted much of Sander's artsy effects. At this three-level flagship store
you also find the men's line that has been given an injection of street
and outgoing elements.

121. Louis Vuitton - French Luxury Leather and Clothes

54, avenue Montaigne   M° Franklin-D.Roosevelt
01 45 62 47 00   Mon-Sat 10.00-20.00
A   €€€

For details see no 62 this chapter.

122. Marithé & Francois Girbaud - Denim and Leisurewear

49, av. Franklin D. Roosevelt M° Franklin-D.Roosevelt
01 45 62 49 15 Mon-Sat 10.00-19.00
M W €€

For details see Étienne Marcel – Les Halles.

9

Opéra

With two of the world's top department stores, most tourists end up here sooner or later.

Here, tons of fashion are concentrated in one small spot which makes shopping convenient and chaotic at the same time. Add to that the famous Garnier Opera House and two of the busiest transport centres in the city, and you'll pretty much understand that this is not the place for relaxation.

Both Galeries Lafayette and Printemps have smartened up considerably over recent years, not least when it comes to men's fashion and sportswear. Sports' clientele will also find the new trainers palace, Citadium a good point of reference – it's a worthy competitor for its counterparts around Les Halles.

Besides the big department stores the area around the Opéra Garnier is dominated by boulevards and streets which all seem to lead to other fashion centres. Boulevard des Capucines is definitely worth taking a walk when heading towards Place de la Madeleine; as is Rue de la Paix on the way to Place Vendôme. While Rue de la Paix is dominated by jewellers and fine accessories shops, Boulevard des Capucines offers high-street fashion.

For wining and dining, Opéra is somewhat of a vacuum. Surrounded by lively nightclub areas nothing seems to have been left in this part of the city. However, for a classic French café, try Café de la Paix.

Eating and drinking

Galeries Lafayette
48, bd Haussmann

Lunch on the roof terrace isn't maybe a gourmet experience but it's hard to find a better setting a sunny day.

Café de la Paix
12, bd des Capucines
01 40 07 30 20

One of the brasserie classics in Paris.

Staying

Pavillon de Paris
7 rue de Parme
www.pavillondeparis.com
01 55 31 60 00

The business person's choice if you should trust the appliances in the rooms - fax/copy machine, internet connection and internet-enabled TV. Still the rooms are well furnished, in a contemporary style. And they are "right-sized" which really isn't the rule in Paris.

Rue des Mathurins
1. Du Pareil au Même

Rue Vignon
2. Paraboot

Rue Godot de Mauroy
3. Annexe de Créateurs

Boulevard de la Madeleine
4. Madelios
5. BCBG
6. Mandarina Duck

Boulevard des Capucines
7. Lacoste
8. Bally
9. Zara
10. Mango

Rue de la Paix
11. Ermenegildo Zegna

12. Repetto
13. Tartine et Chocolat

Rue Auber
14. Muji

Rue Halévy
15. Zara

Avenue de l'Opéra
16. Hugo Boss Woman
17. Hugo Boss

Boulevard Haussmann
18. Galeries Lafayette
19. H&M
20. Printemps

Rue Caumartin
21. Citadium

Rue Saint Lazare
22. H&M

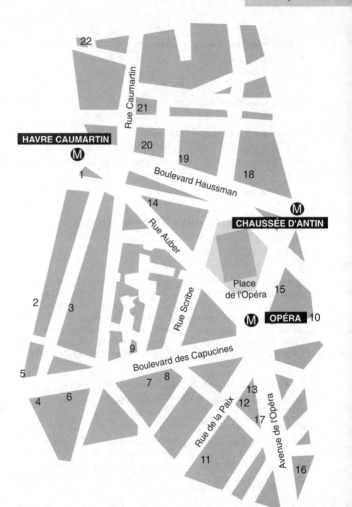

1. Du Pareil au Même - Children's Clothes

15-17, rue des Mathurins   M° Havre Caumartin
01 42 66 93 80   Mon-Sat 10.00-19.00
C   €€

For details see Étienne Marcel - Les Halles.

2. Paraboot - Classic Footwear

13, rue Vignon   M° Madeleine
01 47 22 55 05   Mon 14-19, Tue-Sat 10-19
M W   €€

For details see St-Germain.

3. Annexe de Créateurs - Designer Sale Shop

19, rue Godot de Mauroy   M° Madeleine
01 42 65 46 40   Mon-Sat 11.30-19.00
A M W   €€

At this designer solderie (French for designer sale shop) you find new clothes from same season, last year. Prices are cut by 40-70 percent, the stock changes from week to week but you always find French, Italian and Japanese labels such as Helmut Lang, Dolce Gabbana and Galliano. Labels are left in. There are two shops next to each other, one for day wear and a small selection of menswear, the other for evening and occasion wear. They also have lots of accessories like bags, jewellery and sunglasses.

4. Madelios - International Designer Menswear

23, bd de la Madeleine   M° Madeleine
01 53 45 00 00   Mon-Sat 10.00-19.00
M   €€€

For convenient one-stop shopping the new Madelios offers 4,500 square-metres of high-end designer menswear. Not the most cutting-edge in town, the selection aims at a more conservative but fashion-aware clientele. For cool formal and casual wear you have YSL, Dirk Bikkembergs, Paul Smith, Helmut Lang, Givenchy and Comme des Garçons. For hunting and shooting go for Holland & Holland and Barbour.

5. BCBG - Trend Men and Womenswear

14, boulevard de la Madeleine   M° Madeleine
01 43 26 73 16   Mon-Sat 10.00-19.30
M W   €€

Since its start in 1989 Max Azria's concept of fashionable clothes at sensible prices has been a big success. The label is named BCBG after the phrase Bon Chic Bon Genre meaning "god style, good attitude" – synonymous with bourgeois good taste. Following the trends of the moment the look is for modern women wanting trendy clothes without a certain designers personal imprint - and pricetag. For men the formula is much the same with trendy but not too daring pieces. *Also at: 66, rue Bonaparte (St-Germain), 412, rue St-Honoré (St-Honoré).*

6. Mandarina Duck - Modern Bags & Clothes

7, boulevard de la Madeleine   M° Madeleine
01 42 86 08 00   Mon-Sat 10.00-19.00
A   €€

For details see Montaigne – Fbg St-Honoré.

7. Lacoste - French Sports and Leisure Wear

37, boulevard des Capucines   M° Opéra
01 42 61 58 20   Mon-Sat 10.00-19.00
M W   €€

For details see Montaigne – Fbg St-Honoré.

8. Bally - Urban Chic Shoes, Accessories and Clothes

35, boulevard des Capucines   M° Opéra
01 44 55 38 20   Mon-Sat 10.00-19.00
A M W   €€€

In 1999, the new owners together with creative director Scott Fellows, set out to breathe new life into the 150 year old leather goods house. The intention was, and is, to create a new luxury brand alongside Gucci, Louis Vuitton and the like. The new Bally stands for wearable chic and sleek design with a sporty edge. The brand now also comprises men and womenswear. This is the Parisian flagship store. *Also at: 45, rue Sèvres, 146, avenue des Champs-Elysées.*

9. Zara - Spanish High-Street Fashion

18, boulevard des Capucines   M° Opéra
01 42 68 31 10   Mon-Sat 10.00-19.30
A C M W   €

For details see Étienne Marcel – Les Halles.

10. Mango - High-Street Fashion

6, boulevard des Capucines   M° Opéra
01 53 30 82 70   Mon-Sat 10.00-20.30
A W   €

For details see Étienne Marcel – Les Halles.

11. Ermenegildo Zegna - Italian Tailoring

10, rue de la Paix   M° Opéra
01 42 61 67 61   Mon-Sat 10.00-19.00
M   €€€

For details see Montaigne – Fbg St-Honoré.

12. Repetto - Dancewear

22, rue de la Paix   M° Opéra
01 44 71 83 12   Mon-Sat 10.00-19.00
W   €€

This is a shop selling mainly dancewear, but besides the tutus, leotards and pointy shoes, you also find a good selection of swimwear.

The styles come in different cuts and shapes and they are very reasonable priced (from around €27).

13. Tartine et Chocolat - Children's Clothes

24, rue de la Paix   M° Opéra
01 47 42 10 68   Mon-Sat 10.00-19.00
C   €€

Catherine Painvin's company is a big success. Her up-market children's clothes are cute and polished, but still practical enough to last more than half an hour's wear. The selection of clothes for boys is good compared to many other labels. There is also a range of toys, children's furniture and perfumes. *Also at: 266, boulevard Saint Germain, 22, rue Boissy d'Anglas, 105, rue du Faubourg Saint Honoré, 60, avenue Paul Doumer.*

14. Muji - Japanese Basics

9, rue Auber   M° Opéra
01 43 12 54 00   Mon-Sat 10.00-19.00
A B M O W   €

For details see St-Germain.

15. Zara - Spanish High-Street Fashion

2, rue Halévy   M° Opéra
01 44 71 90 90   Mon-Sat 10.00-20.30
A C M W   €

For details see Étienne Marcel – Les Halles.

16. Hugo Boss Woman - Modern Womenswear

34, avenue de l'Opéra   M° Opéra
01 53 43 05 00   Mon-Sat 10.00-19.30
W   €€

For details see Montaigne – Fbg St-Honoré.

17. Hugo Boss - Modern Menswear

43, avenue de l'Opéra   M° Opéra
01 47 03 94 00   Mon-Sat 10.00-19.30
M   €€

For details see Montaigne – Fbg St-Honoré.

18. Galeries Lafayette - Department Store

48, boulevard Haussmann   M° Chaussèe d'Antin
01 42 82 34 56   Mon-Sat 9.30-6.45, Thu 9.30-21
A B C M O W

This classic Parisian department-store is the most popular among tourists. The seven storeys display brands in every price range from high-street to top-designer labels. Several designer labels have accessories shops, like Prada, Gucci and Dior. The recently revamped menswear building now houses 10,000 square-metres, the largest men's department in Europe. The second floor in the main building is women's designer time with both established and new designers as well as a good selection of high-street labels. The payment system is extremely slow: you pay a cashier and then go back to the salesperson to pick up your purchase. The rooftop terrace on the seventh floor has a breath-taking view over the city. There is also a restaurant.

19. H&M - High-Street Fashion

54, boulevard Haussmann   M° Havre Caumartin
01 55 31 92 50   Mon-Sat 10.00-19.30
A B C M W   €

For details see Étienne Marcel – Les Halles.

20. Printemps - Department Store

64, boulevard Haussmann   M° Havre Caumartin
01 42 82 50 00   Mon-Sat 9.35-19, Thu 9.35-22
A B C M W O

When it comes to fashion, department store Printemps' strongest feature is menswear. The well-edited selection includes all the big like Calvin Klein, YSL and Gucci. For a walk on the wild side, they also stock names like Kostas Mukurdis, Martin Sitbon. Helmut Lang has an in-store shop here. Printemps is actually made up of three separate buildings: Printemps l'Homme for menswear, Printemps de la Maison stocks homewear and children's clothes, and for womenswear it's Printemps de la Mode, where you find a myriad of designers from Balenciaga to Martin Margiela. The lingerie in the basement is also worth checking out.

21. Citadium - Sports and Leisure wear

50-56, rue Caumartin   M° Havre Caumartin
01 55 31 74 00   Mon-Sat 09.30-20,
                            Thu 09.30-21

M W   €€

This gigantic sports and leisure emporium, designed by architect Gerard Barreau, can supply you with almost everything you could possibly want in the fields of sport and camping. Just follow the lines on the floor and you get to the right department. The selection of labels includes all the big names such as Adidas, Nike, Umbro et al. There is also an impressive range of equipment and a selection of cool three-wheel prams.

22. H&M - High-Street Fashion

107, rue Saint Lazare   M° Passage du Havre
01 53 32 87 97   Mon-Sat 10.00-19.30
A B C M W   €

For details see Étienne Marcel – Les Halles.

16

Passy - Victor Hugo

Even though the 16th arrondisement isn't the high-profile fashion area that the sixth and eighth arrondissements are, it still contains more shops than many big European cities.

You come here for a nice shopping experience, with fewer tourists crowding the streets, and a less hectic atmosphere. And for the depôts-vents, which are among the best in Paris.

Basically the shopping in the 16th arrondissement is divided into two separate areas, each with its own identity. In the north east, starting at Place Charles de Gaulle, avenue Victor Hugo and some of the nearby streets offer a bourgeois atmosphere with branches of YSL, Céline and Cerruti 1881. By the Seine the area around Rue du Passy offers a great variety of high-street fashion mixed with more high profile labels such as Joseph and Kenzo.

One reason alone to visit the 16th arrondissement is Franck et Fils, the mini-department store on Rue de Passy. Since it was taken over by LVMH in 1995, it has transformed itself into a fashion heaven, with a great mix of labels such as Marc Jabobs, Sonia Rykiel, APC, Pleats Please, Marcel Maringou and many more.

The most distinguished feature of the 16th is, however, the depôts-vents. The wealthy residents of the area are a never-ending source for second-hand haute couture and ready-to-wear clothes, which several vendors have profited upon. As well as the outstanding Reciproque, which occupies a whole block in Rue de la Pompe, there are also several shops in the area between Rue de Passy and Avenue Victor Hugo.

Eating and drinking

Pré Catelan
route, Suresnes
01 44 14 41 14

Situated in the Bois de Boulogne this is the perfect setting for a outdoor romantic dinner. The food stays in the haute cuisine tradition, and with dishes like the superb scallops in juice of cider the place has earnt itself two stars in the "Rubberman Guide".

Bon
25, rue Pompe
01 40 72 70 00

One of Philippe Starck's latest contributions to the concept restaurant scene. Good food, but, most of all, beautiful guests and environment.

L'Astrance
4, rue Beethoven
01 40 50 84 40

Pascal Barbot's restaurant is a huge success with a contemporary cross-kitchen.

Staying

Pergolèse
3, rue Pergolèse
01 53 64 04 04

Glass, crome and vivid colours are the main ingredients in this modern hotel. Room rates start at €120.

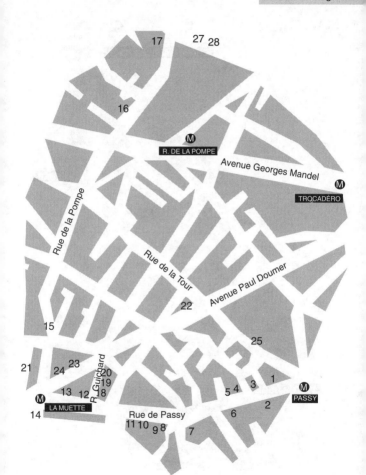

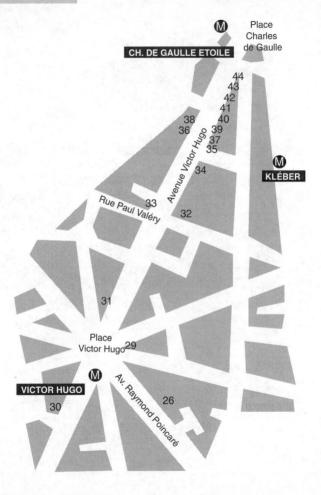

Place
Charles
de Gaulle

CH. DE GAULLE ETOILE

44
43
42
41
40
38   39
36   37
         35
         34
Avenue Victor Hugo

KLÉBER

33
Rue Paul Valéry   32

31

Place
Victor Hugo   29

VICTOR HUGO
30

Av. Raymond Poincaré

26

Rue de Passy
1. Formes
2. Regina Rubens
3. Victoire
4. Zadig & Voltaire
5. Anne Fontaine
6. Joseph
7. Tara Jarmon
8. Zara
9. H&M
10. Camper
11. Etam
12. Et Vous
13. Franck et Fils
14. Kenzo

Rue de la Pompe
15. L'Occaserie 16e
16. Réciproque
17. Chipie

Rue Guichard
18. Eres
19. Le Dépôt-vente de La Muette
20. Scooter

Rue François-Ponsard
21. Dépositif

Avenue Paul Doumer
22. Tartine et Chocolat
23. Ventilo
24. MaxMara

Rue de la Tour
25. Dépôt-Vente de Passy

Avenue Raymond Poincaré
26. Bon Point

Rue Gustave-Courbet
27. Corrine Sarrut
28. Comptoirs des Cottoniers

Place Victor Hugo
29. Francesco Smalto

Avenue Victor Hugo
30. Lacoste
31. Petit Bateau
32. Ventilo
33. Lolita Lempicka
34. Holland & Holland
35. Georges Rech
36. Stephane Kelian
37. Yves Saint Laurent
38. Robert Clergerie
39. Cerruti 1881
40. Frederic Bellulo
41. Marina Rinaldi
42. Apostrophe
43. Hugo Boss (Woman)
44. Céline

1. Formes - Maternity Wear

4, rue de Passy   M° Passy
01 46 47 50 05   Mon-Sat 10.30-19.00
W   €€

For details see Étienne Marcel - Les Halles.

2. Regina Rubens - Classic Womenswear

15, rue de Passy   M° La Muette
01 45 20 56 56   Mon-Sat 10.00-19.00
W   €€

For details see Montaigne - Fbg St-Honoré.

3. Victoire - Chic Womenswear

16, rue de Passy   M° La Muette
01 42 88 20 84   Mon-Sat 10.00-19.00
W   €€

For details see Étienne Marcel - Les Halles.

4. Zadig & Voltaire - Urban Trendy Womenswear

16 bis, rue de Passy   M° La Muette
01 45 2504 07   Mon 13-19.30, Tue-Sat 10.30-19.30
W   €€

For details see St-Honoré.

5. Anne Fontaine - White shirts for Women

22, rue de Passy   M° Passy
01 40 27 05 58   Mon-Sat 10.30-19.00
W   €€

For details see St-Germain.

6. Joseph - Fashionable Womenswear

27, rue de Passy   M° La Muette
01 45 24 24 32   Mon-Sat 10.00-19.00
W   €€

For details see St-Honoré.

7. Tara Jarmon - Contemporary Womenswear

51, rue de Passy   M° La Muette
01 45 24 65 20   Mon-Sat 10.30-19.00
W   €€

For details see St-Germain.

8. Zara - Spanish High-Street Fashion

53, rue de Passy   M° La Muette
01 45 25 07 00   Mon-Sat 10.00-19.30
A C M W   €

For details see Étienne Marcel - Les Halles.

9. H&M - High-Street Fashion

53, rue de Passy   M° La Muette
01 55 74 79 20   Mon-Sat 10.00-19.30
A B C M W   €

For details see Étienne Marcel - Les Halles.

10. Camper - Casual Footwear

55, rue de Passy   M° La Muette
01 42 88 25 60   Mon-Sat 10.00-19.00
M W   €€

For details see Montaigne - Fbg St-Honoré.

11. Etam - High-Street Womenswear

67, rue de Passy   M° La Muette
01 55 74 00 74   Mon-Sat 10.00-19.00
C L W   €

For details see St-Honoré.

12. Et Vous - Contemporary Womenswear

72, rue de Passy   M° La Muette
01 45 20 47 15   Mon-Sat 10.30-19.00
W   €€

For details see Le Marais.

13. Franck et Fils - Chic Mini-Department Store

80, rue de Passy   M° La Muette
01 44 14 38 00   Mon-Sat 10.00-19.00
A L O W   €€€

Since LVMH took over back in 1995 things have been hotting up considerably at this scaled-down department store. If you want to avoid the tourist crowds at Lafayette and the like, this is the place for that quiet shopping experience you deserve. Make the lingerie department your first stop for La Perla, Wolford and other quality brands. In the fashion department you'll find a good mix of top-designer names – both French and international to tempt you. Dior, Tod's and Chanel have their own in-store shops. They also stock a range of more affordable labels such as Paul & Joe and Isabel Marant. If your credit card is still alive there is also a first-class choice of fragrances.

14. Kenzo - French Designer Wear

99, rue de Passy   M° La Muette
01 42 24 92 92   Mon-Sat 10.00-19.00
A M W   €€€

For details see St-Germain.

15. L'Occaserie 16e - Vintage Designer Clothes

19,30, rue de la Pompe   M° La Muette
01 45 03 17 99   Mon-Sat 10.00-19.00
A M W   €€

Not as famous as Réciproque, L'Occaserie is still an instition in the 16th arrondissement when it comes to secondhand shopping. With five shops (there are also shops at 16 and 21, rue de LÁnnonciation and at 14, rue Jean-Bologne) you will not have any problem to kill a couple of hours here. The range stretches from the classic brands to younger fashion like Joseph and Miu Miu. Unlike many other secondhand stores L'Occaserie 16e stocks menswear.

16. Réciproque - Vintage Designer Clothes

92, 95, 97, 101,123, r. d. l. Pompe M° Rue de la Pompe
01 47 04 30 28   Tue-Fri 11-19,
                                Sat 10.30-19.30
A M W   €€

If second-hand designer clothing is what you're into, Réciproque is an absolute must. Six boutiques stretching along the street have all the top prestigious French and international labels such as Hermès, Yves Saint Laurent, Chanel, Prada and Armani. The boutiques stock clothes for every occasion, as well as menswear and accessories, all in good condition. Expect to pay about half the original price tag and make sure you have a couple of hours to spend here, you will need it!

17. Chipie - Preppy Girlswear

129, rue de la Pompe   M° Rue de la Pompe
01 47 27 60 01   Mon 11-19,Tue-Sat 10-19,
                                Lunch 13-14 except Wed, Sat
A C W   €€

Pre-teens love the preppy cool style of Chipie. Their trademark Scottie dog can be found on practically everything from socks and t-shirts to shoes and sweaters. Even the funny nylon bags and accessories continue the theme. The label also includes smaller sizes for younger girls and a few pieces for women.

18. Eres - Sophisticated Swimwear and Lingerie

6, rue Guichard   M° La Muette
01 46 47 45 21   Mon-Sat 10.00-19.00
L W   €€€

For details see Fbg St-Honoré - Montaigne.

19. Le Dépot-vente de La Muette - Vintage Clothes

10, rue Guichard   M° La Muette
01 40 50 79 50   Tue-Sat 11.00-19.00
A W   €€
This is not an ordinary secondhand shop as the clothes are purchased by
the shop and not left in "depôt". However this does not mean that much
for the buyer who can choose from a wide range of used luxury clothes
and accesories. All the goodies are there: YSL, Gucci, Hermès, Prada. They
also stock jewellery from brands such as Chanel and Swarovski.

20. Scooter - Trend Jewellery

12, rue Guichard   M° La Muette
01 45 20 23 27   Mon-Fri 10-19, Sat 11-19
A   €

For details see Étienne Marcel - Les Halles.

21. Dépositif - Vintage Designer Clothes

5, rue François-Ponsard   M° La Muette
01 42 24 10 55   Tue-Sat 10.30-19.00
C   €€

Here you'll find a range of secondhand fashion from not only classic haute couture houses but also more contemporary brands such as
Dries van Noten, Ann Demeulemeester, Gaultier and Vivienne Westwood.

22. Tartine et Chocolat - Children's Clothes

avenue Paul Doumer   M° La Muette
01 45 04 08 94   Mon-Sat 10.00-19.00
C   €€

For details see Opéra.

23. Ventilo - French Classic Womenswear

96, avenue Paul Doumer   M° La Muette
01 40 50 02 21   Mon-Sat 10.30-19.30
W   €€

For details see Étienne Marcel - Les Halles.

24. MaxMara - Italian Elegant Womenswear

100, avenue Paul Doumer   M° La Muette
01 40 50 34 05   Mon-Sat 10.30-19.00
W   €€

For details see Montaigne - Fbg St-Honoré.

25. Dépôt-Vente de Passy - Secondhand Clothes

12-14, rue de la Tour   M° Passy
01 45 20 95 21   Mon 14-19, Tue-Sat 10-19
A W   €€

This secondhand shop focuses on French ready-to-wear from designer labels like Ungaro, Lacroix, YSL and Chanel. You'll also find international designer names like Jil Sander and Armani. There are a lot of accessories like bags, scarves, jewellery and belts too. Expect to pay about a third of the original price.

26. Bon Point – Children's Clothes

60,64, av. Raymond Poincaré M° Victor Hugo
01 44 05 99 8   Mon-Sat 10.00-19.00
C   €€

For details see Étienne Marcel - Les Halles.

27. Corrine Sarrut - Pretty Womenswear

7, rue Gustave-Courbet   M° Victor Hugo
01 55 73 09 73   Mon-Sat 10.00-19.00
W   €€

For details see St-Germain.

28. Comptoir des Cotonniers - Basics

11, rue Gustave-Courbet   M° Victor Hugo
01 45 05 13 55   Mon-Sat 10.00-19.00
W   €

For details see St-Germain.

29. Francesco Smalto - Tailored Menswear

5, place Victor Hugo   M° Victor Hugo
01 45 00 48 64   Mon-Sat 10.00-19.00
M   €€€

For details see the Montaigne - Fbg St-Honoré.

30. Lacoste - French Sports and Leisurewear

92, avenue Victor Hugo   M° Victor Hugo
01 45 53 39 49   Mon-Sat 10.00-19.00
M W   €€

For details see Montaigne - Fbg St-Honoré.

31. Petit Bateau – Children's Clothes and Womens t-shirts

64, avenue Victor Hugo   M° Victor Hugo
01 45 00 13 95   Mon-Sat 10.00-19.00
C W   €

For details see St-Germain.

32. Ventilo - French Classic Womenswear

49, avenue Victor Hugo   M° Victor Hugo
01 40 67 11 01   Mon-Sat 10.30-19.00
W   €€

For details see Étienne Marcel - Les Halles.

33. Lolita Lempicka - Fanciful Designer Wear

46, avenue Victor Hugo   M° Victor Hugo
01 45 02 14 46   Mon 14.30-19,
                                Tue-Sat 10.30-13.30, 14.30-19
W   €€€

For details see Montaigne - Fbg St-Honoré.

34. Holland & Holland - Classic Leisurewear

29, avenue Victor Hugo   M° Victor Hugo
01 45 02 22 00   Mon-Sat 10.00-19.30
A M O W   €€€

Founded in 1835 by Harris Holland, this is where you get that upper
class country and safari clothing that Prince Charles and the like go
for. The women's line has the widest choice, with the traditional hunting look complemented with a modern collection of leather dresses
and leisurewear, far more urban than one might expect. For men the
order is restored with sports jackets, car coats and hunting gear.

35. Georges Rech - French Chic

23, 27, avenue Victor Hugo   M° Victor Hugo
01 45 00 83 19   Mon-Sat 10.00-19.00
M W   €€€

For details see Montaigne - Fbg St-Honoré.

36. Stephane Kelian - Fashionable Shoes

20, avenue Victor Hugo   M° Victor Hugo
01 45 00 44 41   Mon-Sat 10.00-19.00
M W   €€€

For details see St-Germain.

37. Yves Saint Laurent - French Designer

19, avenue Victor Hugo   M° Victor Hugo
01 45 00 64 64   Mon 11-19,
                                Tue-Sat 10.30-19
A W   €€€

For further details see St-Germain.

38. Robert Clergerie - French Designer Shoes

18, avenue Victor Hugo   M° Victor Hugo
01 45 01 81 30   Mon-Sat 10.00-19.00
M W   €€€

For details see St-Germain.

39. Cerrutti 1881 - Italian Design Wear

17, avenue Victor Hugo   M° Victor Hugo
01 53 00 92 61   Mon 11-19,
                                Tue-Sat 10-19
W   €€€

For details see St-Germain.

40. Frederic Bellulo - Elegant Evening Wear

15, avenue Victor Hugo   M° Victor Hugo
01 44 17 96 49   Mon-Sat 10.00-19.00
W   €€€

Step down into what looks like a designers studio and throw your-self into this heaven of elegant party dresses and ball gowns. Lacroix, Mugler, Angelo Tarlazzi, Ungaro, Valentino and Variation by YSL are all lined up together with Bellulo's own designs.

41. Marina Rinaldi - Generous-sized Fashion

7, avenue Victor Hugo   M° Victor Hugo
01 45 01 77 35   Mon-Sat 11.00-19.00
W   €€

For information see St-Germain.

42. Apostrophe – Elegant French Fashion

5, avenue Victor Hugo   M° Victor Hugo
01 45 01 66 91   Mon-Sat 10.00-19.00
W   €€

For information see Montaigne - Fbg St-Honoré

43. Hugo Boss - Fashionable Womenswear

3, avenue Victor Hugo   M° Charles-de-Gaulle Etoile
01 45 02 88 90   Mon-Sat 10.00-19.30
W   €€

For details see Montaigne - Fbg St-Honoré

44. Céline - French Chic

3, avenue Victor Hugo   M° Victor Hugo
01 45 01 80 01   Mon-Sat 10.00-19.00
A W   €€€

For details see the Montaigne - Fbg St-Honoré.

10 11 12 18

Other Destinations

Paris fashion is not only about haute couture and prestigious international designerwear.

This is also where you can find young or unestablished designers, taking their first steps towards a hopefully brilliant career. In recent years clusters of young designer's shops have emerged, mainly concentrated in the north and the east of Paris. Originally many of these areas were the location for a few established designers whose shops attracted customers from the whole city. Antoine et Lili by the Canal St-Martin, Jean Paul Gaultier and Isabel Marrant by the Bastille are the best examples.

The best-developed area is the Bastille where several shops have clustered in the streets Rue de la Charonne, Rue Keller and Rue Faubourg St Antoine. Several new designers have their own boutiques and some fashion media companies have their offices here, which contributes to the funky fashion atmosphere.

Also by the Canal St-Martin, north of Place de la République, young designers have gathered. The stores that attract most customers are Stella Cadente, and the original Antoine et Lili shop with an in-store Salon de thé. This is also a good treat for a Sunday visit, as several boutiques stay open.

Right in between these areas you find Oberkampf, which, besides obvious outlets such as Ursule Beaugeste and the newly opened N° 44, is the place for small interior design boutiques.

There is also exciting, new fashion to explore in the 18th arrondisement, only a stone's throw from the tourist herds in Place de Têtre. Independent designers, as well as some attractive multibrand stores, have gathered around the mètro station Abbesses, and more is to come.

It's worth bearing in mind, that these areas are changing very quickly. Ask the staff in the shops for new openings in the area and you will certainly find that there a several addresses to add to this chapter. That's another thing making these areas so fun.

Eating and drinking

Pause Café Bastille
41, rue Charonne

Mingle with musicians, media types and other bo-bo Parisians.

Cithea
114, rue Oberkamp
01 43 57 55 13

A club for world music and jazz lovers. Live-concerts almost every night.

Bali Bar
9, rue St-Sabin
01 47 00 25 47

For tasty Thai food this is a good bet.

Sardegna a Tavola
1, rue de Cotte
01 44 75 03 28

If you have spent to much on your shopping tour this Sardinian restaurant delivers good-valued rustic Italian food like ravoli stuffed with ricotta and mushrooms in delicous tomato sauce.

Les Fernandises
19, rue de la Fontaine-au-Roi
01 48 06 16 96

If cheese makes you smile, this is the place to go. The kitchen delivers good dishes in the French tradition.

China Club
50, rue de Charenton
01 43 43 82 02

With a glamorous, relaxed atmosphere this is the perfecet setting for sipping Cosmopolitans.

Staying

Hôtel Beaumarchais
3 rue Oberkampf
01 53 36 86 86
www.hotelbeaumarchais.com

An IKEA-furnished low-priced hotel in the party quarter of Oberkampf. A great example of how even less expensive hotels can be well-styled. Doubles cost about €90.

La Manufacture
8, rue Phillippe de Champagne
01 45 35 45 25

For a stylish stay at affordable prices this is a good bet. Doubles from €128. 15 minutes to the Orly airport.

Bastille
Passage Charles-Dallery
1. Ladies and Gentlemen
2. Sandrine Leonard

Rue de Charonne
3. Be.You. (K)
4. Geda. E-pure
5. Isabel Marrant
6. Jellypot
7. Shine
8. Ekdotin
9. La Sartan
10. Catherine Magnan

Rue Keller
11. Gravity Zero
12. Des Petit Hautes by Éroé
13. Anne Willi
14. Le Dix Huit

Rue des Taillandiers
15. Tosca
16. Espace Bastille

Rue Fbg Saint Antoine
17. Etam
18. Galerie Gaultier
19. Carhartt
20. Lacoste

Rue Saint Nicolas
21. Louison
22. Accostages

Rue Faidherbe
23. Catalys

Oberkampf
Rue Oberkampf
24. Ursule Beaugeste

Rue Jean Pierre Timbaud
25. N°44

Rue de Nemours
26. Sissi Holleis

République
Quai de Valmy
27. Stella Cadente
28. Antoine et Lili, Le Village

Rue Beaurepaire
29. Liza Korn
30. Ginger et Lily

Rue Dieu
31. Agnès B.

Abbesses
Rue des Abbesses
32. Bonnie Cox

Rue la Vieuville
33. Spree
34. Lili Perpink

Rue des Martyrs
35. Heaven

Rue Houdon
36. Patricia Lousior
37. FutureWare Lab

Rue Yvonee Le Tac
38. Gaspard de la Butte

Rue Burq
39. La Boutique Tibetaine

Boulevard de Rochechouart
40. Tati
41. Guerrisold

Not on map

42. Jamin Puech, 10th
43. Hortensia Louisor, 9th
44. E2, 10th
45. L'Atrium, 17th
46. L'Espionne, 17th

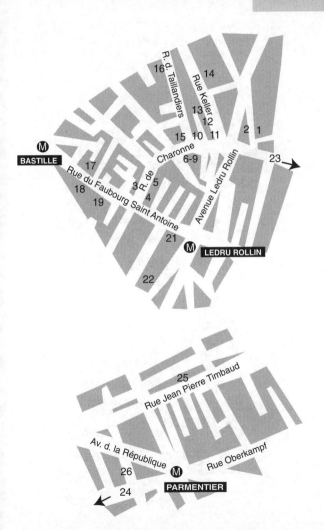

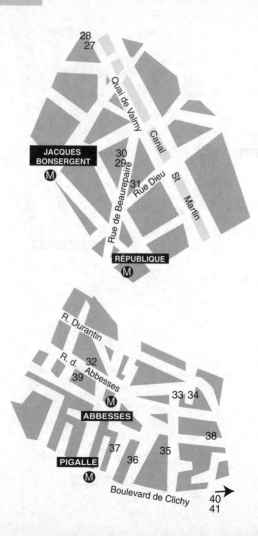

1. Ladies and Gentlemen - Trendy Design Wear

4, passage Charles-Dallery   M° Voltaire
01 47 00 86 12   Tue-Sat 12-19 Sun 14-19
M W   €€

Two young designers, Isabelle Ballu and Moritz Rogosky, have come together forming this hip boutique. Rogosky designs colourful menswear that suits the trendy laid-back playboy, with loose hanging striped shirts and slim-fitting trousers. Soft suits and long overcoats in jersey complete the look. Ballu who does the womenswear, keeps it simple but sophisticated with a sober palette of black and white. It's a modern, cool yet feminine look with clean shapes and great attention to detail.

2.Sandrine Leonard - Handbags and Accessories

5, passage Charles-Dallery   M° Voltaire
01 47 00 09 94   Tue-Sat 14.00-19.00
A   €€

The Toulouse-based Sandrine Leonard now has her own Paris boutique where she sells a wide range of her bags in different styles, sizes and fabrics. There's a basic range of clean, no fuss nylon bags that come in a rainbow of colours. Another line is more frivolous with big flower prints in bold colours. Good value for money.

3. Be.You.(K) - Funky Club Wear

7-9, rue de Charonne   M° Ledru-Rollin
01 40 21 02 20   Mon 14-20, Tue-Sat 11-20
W   €€

The clothes from this Bordeaux-based label have a strong club flavour for young party girls who want to have a ball. Denim is a staple fabric with trousers, long skirts and embroidered skirts. The red velour trousers are a winner. Complete the look with small tank tops in different cuts and prints and you're ready to rock. *Also at: 150, Bld Saint Germain (St-Germain).*

4. Geda. E-pure - Streetwear

8, rue de Charonne	M° Ledru-Rollin
01 47 00 42 75	Mon 14-19.30,
	Tue-Sat 11-19.30
M W	€€

In this cool plywood panelled boutique find French street-wear label Geda. E-pure. On display are well-priced urban smart-looking clothes with sportswear and club influences for street-savvy girls and boys. *Also at: 101, rue de Seine (St-Germain), 3, rue d'Argout (Étienne Marcel-Les Halles)*

5. Isabel Marant - Bohemian-Chic Womenswear

16, rue de Charonne	M° Ledru-Rollin
01 49 29 71 55	Mon-Sat 10.30-19.30
A W	€€

Young French designer Isabel Marant is a must for every Parisian boho-girl. Her look is easy to recognise, with a mix of past and present, and a variety of ethnic African and Indian influences. It's a funky cheap-chic style with natural fabrics and cuts that mould the body without constricting it, as seen in blanket-like coats or knit-cardigans. Marant also does her own line of jewellery and bags. This is the largest shop in Paris. *Also at: 1, rue Jacob (St-Germain)*

6. Jellypot - Sporty Streetwear

28-30, rue de Charonne	M° Ledru-Rollin
01 48 06 55 66	Mon-Sat 11.30-20.00
M W	€€

This is actually two shops that sell men and women's streetwear respectively. The mix of labels such as Carhartt, Triple Soul and North Face stands for a sporty urban vibe that will definitely take you through the city jungle. Womenswear also includes tank tops and cute dresses. The suitably casual footwear comes from Coq Sportif, Clarks and Birkenstock etc.

7. Shine - International Designer Wear

30, rue de Charonne   M° Ledru-Rollin
01 48 05 80 10   Mon-Sat 11.00-19.30
A W   €€€

A must when looking for cutting-edge young designers. Italian owner Vinci D'Elia's mix of hot labels is regarded by some as a groovier alternative to Maria Luisa's selection. The overall look is sophisticated funky 1980s. Spice up your wardrobe with labels such as English Blaak, Sophia Malig and Preen or go American with Earl Jean and Diane Furstenberg. Francophiles can catch Laurent Mercier and Cacharel. Love the black wallpaper with golden bamboo print.

8. Ekdotin - Streetwear

30, rue de Charonne   M° Ledru-Rollin
01 43 14 06 39   Mon-Sat 10.30-19.30
C W   €€

Designer Carole Bigielman does street-influenced clothes for hip Bastille girls looking for that party-night outfit. But unlike many other club-wear labels her jeans and tops don't just work for babes under 20. You can also check out the WOWO-label that does bright children's clothes.

9. La Sartan - Fashionable Hats and Bags

30, rue de Charonne   M° Ledru-Rollin
01 43 38 81 16   Tue-Sat 12.00-20.00
A   €€

Fabienne Laurent, from the south of France, creates hats with a casual look that will make the non hat-wearer think twice. There are two main styles, neither has that extravagant big drama look that seldom fits into everyday life. Perhaps that's why the Japanese are crazy about them. They all come in fabrics with gorgeous prints, florals, stripes or ethnically-inspired. The same fabrics are used to make the pretty bags. Laurent also makes hats for Joseph.

10. Catherine Magnan - Sophisticated Clubwear

39, rue de Charonne   M° Ledru-Rollin
01 43 55 56 57   Mon-Sat 11.00-19.30
W   €€

In this studio-cum-boutique former Plein Sud co-worker, Catherine Magnan creates her urban womenswear. The clothes come with feminine silhouettes in new fabrics with black, white and red as the preferred colours. She gives the clothes a modern street-tough feeling by slashing and tearing the fabric and by spray-painting bold prints on the pieces.

11. Gravity Zero - Clubwear

1, rue Keller   M° Ledru-Rollin
01 43 57 97 62   Mon 13-20, Tue-Sat 11-20
M W O   €€

Unlike most concept-stores, Gravity Zero is aimed at the young-minded clubbers. The store isn't big but it manages to display an array of lifestyle articles without feeling cramped. The style is "ethnic flavours meets cyber aesthetics" as seen in clothes and accessories from different young designers. There is also a selection of CDs and small objets d'art.

12. Des Petit Hautes by Éroé - Women's Tops

11, rue Keller   M° Ledru-Rollin
01 43 57 58 48   Tue-Sat 11.45-19.15
A W   €€

This shop is all about tops in different shapes and vivid colours. Sisters Katia and Vanessa Sanchez are the brains behind the designs that come in clean-cut simple shapes. They play with detailing in a discreet but appealing way may it be small pockets, embroidery or buttons. The preferred fabrics are cotton, linen and polyester. There is also a small range of cute handbags, jewellery, gloves and belts.

13. Anne Willi - Sober Feminine Womenswear

13, Rue Keller   M° Ledru-Rollin
01 48 06 74 06   Mon 14-20,
       Tue-Sat 11.30-20
W   €€

After six years in Tel Aviv, Anne Willi was one of the first young
designers to establish her business in Rue Keller. Here she offers
well-composed collections in a sober and feminine style. Prices are
very competitive, and if you are looking for something really wearable but still with a personal touch, this is a label for you.

14. Le Dix Huit - Young Designers

18, rue Keller   M° Ledru-Rollin
01 43 38 81 16   Mon-Sat 12.00-19.00
A M O W   €€

In this boutique-cum-showroom, young designers display and sell
their creations. The overall theme changes every couple of months.
There is also a selection of accessories and knick-knacks.

15. Tosca - Vintage Women's Clothing

1, rue des Taillandiers   M° Bastille
01 48 06 71 24   Tue-Sat 14.00-19.00
A W   €€

This is not about old designer clothes or couture findings. What
makes this a must for second-hand hunters is the superb choice of
period clothing from 1900 to the 1970s. Owner Tonia changes the
collection to fit the trends and seasons. The prices are reasonable,
something that cannot be taken for granted after recent years' craze
for anything "vintage". Accessories are also a good bet. Wedding
dresses and more expensive items can be viewed by appointment.

16. Espace Bastille - Young Designers

27, rue Taillandiers   M° Bastille
01 43 55 22 89   Mon-Sat 12.00-19.30
M W O   €

Young designers not only sell their creations here, they can also use the owners' sewing machines and other equipment. In the large three-storey shop, which looks like a flea market, you find clothes, accessories and furniture. Younger ones share space with established designers for an unlimited style mix that includes New York Industrie, Westwood Red label, Moloko, Mü, Des Habits, Solola, Entrace and many more.

17. Etam - High-Street Womenswear

13, rue du Fbg Saint Antoine   M° Bastille
01 56 95 06 44   Mon-Sat 10.00-19.00
C L W   €

For details see the Étienne Marcel - Les Halles.

18. Galerie Gaultier - French Couturier

30, rue du Fbg Saint Antoine   M° Bastille
01 44 68 84 84   Mon, Sat 11-19,
                             Tue-Fri 10.30-19.30
A M W   €€€

Former 'enfant terrible' of French fashion, Jean Paul Gaultier is still one of the most influential designers. Since he started his label in 1978 he has created clothes with an eclectic mix of street and ethnic influences, brilliant tailoring and an overall funky sense of humour. Sexual ambiguity has also been a theme in his designs with men dressed in skirts and women in pin-striped business suits. At this store you'll find all the different lines, as well as less expensive JPG Jeans and loads of accessories and perfumes. *Also at: 6, Galerie Vivienne (Étienne Marcel - Les Halles).*

19. Carhartt - Streetwear

38bis, rue du Fbg St-Antoine   M° Bastille
01 40 02 02 20   Mon-Sat 10.30-19.00
M W   €€

In this airy, newly-opened shop, you'll find a large range of urban street and workwear from American label Carhartt. In 1889 the company started making durable work clothes. A hundred years later, black rap-music group N.W.A. launched their now classic album "Straight outta Compton", wearing the full Carhartt equipment. After that the label found its way into many street-smart artists' wardrobes. Even today mainstream celebs like Bruce Willis and Kevin Costner have been seen wearing Carhartt in recent movies.

20. Lacoste - French Sports and Leisurewear

70-72, rue du Fbg St-Antoine   M° Bastille
01 43 45 03 09   Mon-Sat 10.00-19.00
M W   €€

For details see the Montaigne - Fbg St-Honoré.

21. Louison - Fashionable Accessories

20, rue Saint Nicolas   M° Ledru-Rollin
01 43 44 02 62   Mon-Sat 11.00-19.00
A W   €€

The accessories and shoes from the label Louison have a fashionable yet personal look. The handbags and shoes that are chic and functional always come with detailing that give them that extra something, like the range of canvas bags in natural colours with technicolour leather detail-trim. The duo behind the label is Agnès and Jaques Choi. Jaques is the designer, and before the couple launched their own label in 1998, he worked for labels like Tod's and Hogan. Both the handbags and shoes are reasonably priced.

22. Accostages - Innovative Fabrics

3, rue Saint Nicolas   M° Ledru-Rollin
01 44 87 03 36   Tue-Fri 11-19, Sat 13-19
O W   €€

The fabrics are what make Accostage special. French-Greek designer Sophie Bastais creates clothes and decoration collections using innovative materials like cotton that changes colour when you touch it, or fabric mixed with steel thread. Light and airy the fabrics materialize into "friendly clothes" with a loose silhouette and a slightly bohemian mood. The styles are versatile and come with details such as raw-cut, fringes and drawstrings.

23. Catalys - Young Designers' Collective

40, rue Faidherbe   M° Faidherbe
06 80 64 56 85   Mon-Sat 11.00-19.00
C M W   €€

Off the beaten fashion track this designers' collective displays a wide range of young unestablished French designers. Latifa, Clément & Caposella and a dozen more labels in as many styles that ranges from ultra-feminine neat black silk pieces to workwear-inspired boxy outfits in thick fabrics. Contrary to what one might expect, most of the clothes are wearable, not conceptual "more art than real life fashion" but still with a personal expression to them.

24. Ursule Beaugeste - Fashionable Accessories

15, rue Oberkampf   M° Filles du Calvaire
01 48 06 71 09   Tue-Fri 11-19, Sat 11.30-19
A   €€

Since the first collection hit the streets in 1992, Ursule Beaugeste has been a name in the fashion world. Anne Grand-Clément, the woman behind the label, and former shoe designer for Cerrutti and Sonia Rykiel, creates exquiste handbags in a sober cosmopolitan style. Her collections include openwork raffia bags, engraved ethnic patterns on leather totes, and army-like wool-felt messenger bags. The well-priced bags are also functional and if you want something that's not on everybody's arm this is a good bet. She also does beautifully stitched gloves and beaded purses.

25. N°44 - Lifestyle and Fashion

59, rue Jean Pierre Timbaud   M° Parmentier
01 56 98 18 44   Mon-Sat 13.00-21.00
A M O W   €€

A lifestyle-store created by Japanese Seiichiro Shimamura, N°44 sells a contemporary mix of clothes, music, shoes, accessories, candles and other small items by different designers, although it mainly stocks its own label, 0044. Their collections focuses on basics that have a strong utility look, taking inspiration from army and workwear. Items could be made out of fabric from a German army tent for example.

26. Sissi Holleis - Fashionable Womenswear

3,rue de Nemours   M° Parmentier
01 43 38 10 71   Mon-Sat 10.30-19.30
A W   €€

Young Austrian designer Sissi Holleis does pretty feminine clothes with a rock-gothic edge that groovy Parisians in search of labels with attitude come here for. She worked at fashion houses such as Karl Lagerfeld and Guy Laroche before opening this studio-cum-boutique with black lacquer and oversized chandeliers. You also will find shoes by Japanese AKA and Italian Quelle, as well as jewellery by ANN.

27. Stella Cadente - Romantic Womenswear

93, quai de Valmy   M° Jacques Bonsergent
01 42 09 27 00   Mon-Sun 11.00-19.30
A W   €€

It's a perfect setting at the St-Martin canal for Stella Cadente's charming boutique. Her clothes are ultra-romantic, and with the fairy-like pale pastels, soft fabrics, flounces and beading you can almost imagine yourself floating in a small boat down the canal. The silhouette is gentle and body-conscious, as seen in her dresses or knitwear. She started out as a jewellery designer, and you can still complete your look with her pieces that have the same graceful old-fashioned style.

28. Antoine et Lili, Le Village - Ethnic Hippie Womenswear

95, quai de Valmy
01 40 37 41 55

A M W

M° Jacques Bonsergent
Mon-Fri 11-18, Sat 10-20,
Sun 14-19.30
€€

This kitsch-looking fuschia and banana-yellow shop sells pretty, ethnic-inspired clothes with a "hippie straight out of Woodstock spirit" in colour and fabrics. The clothes, colourful knits and folksy ponchos, are inexpensive. They also stock quirky gifts. They have branches all over Paris, but "Le Village" is the largest store and you'll also find furniture, florist and a salon de thé here. *Also at, amongst others: 51, rue des Francs Bourgeois(Le Marais) 87, rue de Seine (St-Germain).*

29. Liza Korn - Urban Feminine Womenswear

19, rue Beaurepaire
01 42 01 36 02

W

M° République
Tue-Sat 11-19.30,
Sun 14-19.30
€€

Young designer Liza Korn creates feminine clothes with her own personal twist, that gives them an up-dated urban look. She mixes elements of trash with class. She pays great attention to detail and plays with a vast palette of colours.

30. Ginger et Lily - Young Urban Clothes

33, rue Beaurepaire
01 42 06 07 73

A O W

M° République
Tue-Sat 11-19,
Sun 15-19.30
€€

Here, at former fashion journalist Francoise Devos' boutique, things she has collected at her trips around the world are on display. You'll find a mix of different smaller labels and young designers. The look is young and urban, with a strong ethnic flavour. There is also a selection of exotic items, accessories and jewellery.

31. Agnès b. Sport - French Casual Chic

1, rue Dieu   M° République
01 42 03 47 99   Mon-Sat 10.30-19.30
M W   €€

For details see St-Honoré.

32. Bonnie Cox – Urban Womenswear

38, rue des Abbesses   M° Abbesses
01 42 54 95 68   Mon-Sun 11.00-19.00
A W   €€

At Bonnie Cox the style is urban street with a cybernetic flavour. Labels include Fornarina, Legend from Castelbajac, Catherine Magnan and shoes from Kultje, Coq Sportif and Repetto. Her own-label hats are famous.

33. Spree - Trendy Fashion and Furniture

16, rue la Vieuville   M° Abbesses
01 42 23 41 40   Tue-Sat 11-00-19.30
A M W   €€

Tucked away in the 18th arrondissement, far away from the high-density fashion areas, you find this furniture and fashion boutique. The women and children's wear come from designers such as British Preen, Eley Kishimoto, Dirty Youth of UK, French Isabel Marant and the Italian jeans label, Tim Camino – sold exclusively in France. The furniture ranges from the 1930s to the 1970s. The airy store also stocks various small items such as soap, socks and jewellery.

34. Lili Perpink - Young Japanese Fashion

22, rue la Vieuville   M° Abbesses
01 42 52 37 24   Tue-Sat 11.30-19.30
A O W   €€

You certainly don't find this kind of girlie bubble-gum fashion on every street corner. A range of Japanese labels such as Shake your soul, Nice Club and Indio do a sort of twinkle-in-the-eye take on Hello Kitty stuff in neat tops, skirts and an array of knick-knacks. Everything comes in intense candy colours with different kinds of print. In other words, this is as far from the severe Japanese fashion tradition as you can get.

35. Heaven - Designer Wear

83, rue des Martyrs   M° Abbesses
01 44 92 92 92   Tue-Sat 11-19.30
     Sun-Mon 14-19.30
M O W   €€

In this boutique-cum-studio English designer Lea-Ann Wallis creates her individualistic romantic clothes. Some pieces are one-offs, others are made in a small series. The style is youthful and nostalgic in a non-fussy way, but tends to be quite dressed-up. The men's line is casual and artsy-looking with loose silhouettes and low-key colours. Downstairs her husband Jean Christophe makes delicate one-off beaded lamps and chandeliers.

36. Patricia Louisor - Funky Fashion

16, rue Houdon   M° Abbesses
01 42 62 10 42   Daily 12.00-20.00
W   €€

This is a favourite stop for every Pigalle fashion kitten. They come here for Patricia Louisor's clothes with an individual look that mixes Parisian chic with well-dressed bohemian flavours and glittering club vibes. She works with innovative materials and fabrics, and the tailoring is always figure-flattering. Combine this with high quality and cheap prices and you've got a real winner.

37. FutureWare Lab – Avant-garde Dressing

23, rue Houdon M° Pigalle
01 42 23 66 08 Tue-Sat 11-19, Sun 16-19
M W €€

For details see Le Marais.

38. Gaspard de la Butte - Children's Clothes

10, rue Yvonne Le Tac M° Abbesses
01 42 55 99 40 Daily 10.00-19.00
C €€

This is a little treasure trove for wonderful and original clothes for kids under six years. The style is simple, but the clothes are made in unusual fabrics and incorporate really creative details like fanciful buttons and detachable pockets which the kids will love. Many items are reversible which mums will love. Young designers shop here and you won't find the style anywhere else.

39. La boutique Tibetaine - Tibetan Crafts

4, rue Burq M° Abbesses
01 42 59 14 86 Tue-Sat 10.30-19.00
A O W €€

Tibetan folklore and crafts are what it's all about here. Embodied peasant blouses and gowns in dark patterned textiles. Ethnic jewellery with intricate patterns and forms, as well as interior objects, such as statues and lanterns are on display.

40. Tati - Discount Department Store

4, bd de Rochechouart M° Barbès Rouchouart
01 42 55 13 09 Mon 10-19, Tue-Fri 09.30-19,
Sat 09.15-19

A C M O W €

In the capital of luxury and good taste, Tati is synonymous with the opposite. Nylon knickers, bad-taste household ornaments and polyester trousers all come at prices that make every bargain-hunter smile. What started out in 1948 with immigrants and the poor as target customers is today a tourist attraction just like the Eiffel Tower. Now the Tati concept is spreading, both geographically and branch-wise, you can now shop at Tati d'Or for discount jewellery and at Tati Optic for eyewear. *Also at: 13, rue de la Règpublique. Tati d'Or, 19, rue de la Paix, Tati Optic, 11, rue Belhomme.*

41. Guerrisold – Secondhand Clothes

17, bd de Rochechouart M° Anvers
01 45 26 38 92 Mon-Sat 9.30-19.30
A M W €

If you love bargain, trashy fashion and can live without designer labels, this is your place. Guerrisold deals with mass-market second-hand clothes, mostly from the 1970s and 80s. It's cheap and well-organized. The downside is that often you'll find absolutely nothing worth taking home. Then there is the smell, which can be hard to stand. Dry-cleaning your findings is a must. Avoid Mondays as there is nothing left after Saturdays. This and 19, 29, 33 avenue de Clichy are the best branches.

42. Jamin Puech - Fashion Accessories

61, rue d'Hauteville M° Poissonière
01 40 22 08 32 Mon 11-19,
Tue-Sat 9-19

A €€

Benoit Jamin and Isabelle Puechs' stock score an all-time high on the fashion market. Chloé and Lagerfeld have recently sought their assistance, and the fashion glitterati eagerly snap up their fresh lady-like creations. The classic shapes come to life with an unpredictable mix of knitting, crochet, patchwork, shells, embroidery, straw and signature beading. Add to that prices that are lower than the major design labels and the exclusivity-factor.

43. Hortensia Louisor - Maternity and Children's Clothes

14, rue Clauze	M° St Georges
01 45 26 67 68	Mon 14-19.30,
	Tue-Sat 11-20
C W	€€

Caroline and Monique, sister of Patricia Louisor who has her cool shop in Montmartre, bring you fresh urban maternity and kid's clothes. The children's line is unisex up to age three, then it's a girl thing. The look is original with simple but playful pieces in warm colours and with great attention to detail. The maternity clothes are smart and fashionable, with cuts that make the best of your mother-to-be shape.

44. E2 - Customized Vintage Clothes

15, rue Martel	M° Chateau d'Eau
01 47 70 15 14	By appointment only
W	€€€

The E2-label caused a stir in 2001, and Madonna and Gwyneth Paltrow snatched up loads of their made-over vintage clothes. The design duo behind the label is husband and wife Olivier and Michèle Chatenet, they uses flea market finds and vintage couture in the dresses, blouses and skirts, which they reinterpret with a high level of imagination. These customized limited-edition pieces come in an ultra-feminine style.

45. L'Atrium - One-stop Shopping Centre

Palais des Congrès   M° Porte Maillot
                            Mon-Sat 10.30-19.30
A C M O W

In the congress building Palais de Congrès the shopping center L'Atrium provides an impressive range of multi- and mono-label shops. The focus is on mainstream labels such as Hugo Boss, Kenzo, Escada and George Rech.

46. L'Espionne - International Designer Wear

Palais de Congrès   M° Porte Maillot
01 40 68 23 31   Mon-Sat 10.00-19.00
A W M   €€

Quite surprisingly given its location in the Palais de Congrès shopping centre, this ambitious boutique sells a well-edited label mix. You find more cutting-edge names like Jean Paul Knott and jeans label Zoomp, as well as the more established league, like Prada and John Galliano.

Fashion Glossary

Atelier: The studio or workshop of a designer.

Custom-made: Clothes that are made for an individual customer by a tailor or couturier, according to his or her original designs.

Dépôt-Ventes: The shops that sell recent second-hand clothing, come in every price range.

Diffusion line: A designer's second and more affordable line.

Fripe: The French word for second-hand clothing from another decade.

(Haute) Couture: The French word for made-to-measure garments that come with the highest levels of craftsmanship, exclusive fabrics and original styles.

Made-to-measure: Clothes made according to an individual's measurements. No fittings required.

Prêt-a-porter/Ready-to-wear: The French and English expressions for mass manufactured clothes in standard sizes.

Solderie: The French word for sale shop. It's either a shop that sells unsold stock from different designers, or a permanent sale store that offers clothes from a specific label.

Vendeur/Vendeuse: Male and female sales assistant.

Index

Index

Check out www.pulpoguides.com for
up-dates and new releases

Pulpo Guides - your navigator in the
world of travel, fashion, food and lifestyle